**TEACHER'S PET PUBLICATIONS**

LITPLAN TEACHER PACK
for
The Great Gilly Hopkins
based on the book by
Katherine Paterson

Written by
Janine H. Sherman

© 1998 Teacher's Pet Publications
All Rights Reserved

This **LitPlan** for Katherine Paterson's
The Great Gilly Hopkins
has been brought to you by Teacher's Pet Publications, Inc.

Copyright Teacher's Pet Publications 1998
11504 Hammock Point
Berlin MD 21811

Only the student materials in this unit plan (such as worksheets,
study questions, and tests) may be reproduced multiple times
for use in the purchaser's classroom.
No other portion may be reproduced in any form without written
consent from Teacher's Pet Publications, Inc.

For any additional copyright questions,
contact Teacher's Pet Publications.

www.tpet.com

TABLE OF CONTENTS - *The Great Gilly Hopkins*

Introduction	5
Unit Objectives	7
Reading Assignment Sheet	8
Unit Outline	9
Study Questions (Short Answer)	13
Quiz/Study Questions (Multiple Choice)	22
Pre-reading Vocabulary Worksheets	39
Lesson One (Introductory Lesson)	55
Nonfiction Assignment Sheet	62
Oral Reading Evaluation Form	64
Writing Assignment 1	61
Writing Assignment 2	66
Writing Assignment 3	74
Writing Evaluation Form	76
Vocabulary Review Activities	86
Extra Writing Assignments/Discussion ?s	78
Unit Review Activities	88
Unit Tests	91
Unit Resource Materials	133
Vocabulary Resource Materials	149

A FEW NOTES ABOUT THE AUTHOR
Katherine Paterson

PATERSON, Katherine (1932-). Three time Newbery award winning author Katherine Paterson calls herself a gypsy. She has lived in three countries and many states. She doesn't feel she has a home in that sense, so to her, she doesn't have a place out of which stories naturally come.

These sentiments come from an author whose writing in every aspect, not only setting, seems to come very naturally. Characters in Paterson's Newbery Honor book, *The Great Gilly Hopkins* and Newbery Medal novels, *Bridge to Terabithia* and *Jacob Have I Loved* totally belong where they are. And where they are is where she has spent a good part of her life, in the mid-Atlantic region of the United States. These are her recent works, though. Earlier novels: *The Sign of the Chrysanthemum, Of Nightingales That Weep, and The Master Puppeteer* are set in Japan, where she attended and taught school in the 1950's.

She doesn't think you have to fight dragons to write books, but to live deeply the life you've been given. Her deeply -lived life has taken her all over the world. She spent her early childhood in China, where her father was a missionary. During World War II, she was evacuated with her family. They came to live in various parts of Virginia, North Carolina, and West Virginia, where Katherine's odd clothes and British accent made her an outcast. As a result, she became an avid reader with a vivid imagination.

Katherine feels a book always grows out of who you are. You may wish it to be different, you might even pretend it to be different, but she insists the book will betray you. What you are will always come out in the book, she testifies. When asked what qualifies her to be a writer for children, she responds with the fact the she was once a weird little kid. She thinks that gives her a head start.

Katherine has written a total of twelve books including these most recent: *Lyddie* (1991), *The King's Equal* (1992), and *Flip-Flop Girl* (1994). She and her Presbyterian minister husband, John Paterson, have four children who have provided her with much of the subject matter for her keenly observant stories of family life. She presently lives in Barre, Vermont.

INTRODUCTION

This unit has been designed to develop students' reading, writing, thinking, and language skills through exercises and activities related to *The Great Gilly Hopkins* by Katherine Paterson. It includes eighteen lessons, supported by extra resource materials.

The **introductory lesson** introduces students to the topic (foster care) of the novel by Katherine Paterson. Following the introductory activity, students are given the materials they will use during the unit.

The **reading assignments** are approximately twenty-five pages each; some are a little shorter while others are a little longer. Students have approximately 15 minutes of Pre-reading work to do prior to each reading assignment. This pre-reading work involves reviewing the study questions for the assignment and studying 10 vocabulary words the students will encounter in their reading.

The **study guide questions** are fact-based questions; students can find the answers to these questions right in the text. These questions come in two formats: short answer or multiple choice. We suggest that you use the short answer version of the questions as study guides for students (since answers will be more complete), and use the multiple choice version for occasional quizzes. It might be a good idea to make transparencies of your answer keys to use on the overhead projector.

The **vocabulary work** is intended to enrich students' vocabularies as well as to aid in the students' understanding of the book. Prior to each reading assignment, students will complete a two-part worksheet for 10 vocabulary words in the upcoming reading assignment. Part I focuses on students' use of general knowledge and contextual clues by giving the sentence in which the word appears in the text. Students are then to write down what they think the words mean based on the words' usage. Part II nails down the definitions of the words by giving students dictionary definitions of the words and having students match the words to the correct definitions based on the words' contextual usage. Students should then have an understanding of the words when they meet them in the text.

After each reading assignment, students will go back and formulate answers for the study guide questions. Discussion of these questions serves as a **review** of the most important events and ideas presented in the reading assignments.

After students complete extra discussion questions, there is a **vocabulary review** lesson which pulls together all of the fragmented vocabulary lists for the reading assignments and gives students a review of all of the words they have studied.

Following the reading of the book, two lessons are devoted to the **extra discussion questions/writing assignments/activities**. These questions focus on interpretation, critical analysis and personal response, employing a variety of thinking skills and adding to the students' understanding of the novel. These questions are done as a **group activity**. Using the information they have acquired so far through individual work and class discussions, students get together to further examine the text and to brainstorm ideas relating to the themes of the novel.

The group activity is followed by a **reports and discussion/ activity** session in which the groups share their ideas about the book with the entire class; thus, the entire class gets exposed to many different ideas regarding the themes and events of the book.

There are three **writing assignments** in this unit. The first assignment is to inform: students will research racial prejudice and create a poem that depicts ways this intolerance can be combated. The second assignment gives students the opportunity to express their personal ideas: students will design and compose a "missing poster" in which an appeal is made for Gilly's return. The third assignment is to give students a chance to persuade: students pretend to be Maime Trotter trying to convince Gilly to stay with her grandmother.

In addition, there is a **nonfiction reading assignment**. Students are required to read a piece of nonfiction related in some way to *The Great Gilly Hopkins*. After reading their nonfiction pieces, students will fill out a worksheet on which they answer questions regarding facts, interpretation, criticism, and personal opinions. During one class period, students make **oral presentations** about the nonfiction pieces they have read. This not only exposes all students to a wealth of information, it also gives students the opportunity to practice **public speaking**.

Another feature of this unit is the **speaker** day. This provides an extension of the theme of foster care. A professional in this field will be asked to share insight, law, and experiences on this topic.

The **review lesson** pulls together all of the aspects of the unit. The teacher is given four or five choices of activities or games to use which all serve the same basic function of reviewing all of the information presented in the unit.

The **unit test** comes in two formats: all multiple choice-matching-true/false or with a mixture of matching, short answer, and composition. As a convenience, two different tests for each format have been included.

There are additional **support materials** included with this unit. The **unit and vocabulary resource sections** include suggestions for an in-class library, crossword and word search puzzles related to the novel, and extra vocabulary games and worksheets. There is a list of **bulletin board ideas** for the teacher to go along with this unit. In addition, there is a list of **extra class activities** the teacher could choose from to enhance the unit or as a substitution for an exercise the teacher might feel is inappropriate for his or her class. **Answer keys** are located directly after the **reproducible student materials** throughout the unit. The student materials may be reproduced for use in the teacher's classroom without infringement of copyrights. No other portion of this unit may be reproduced without the written consent of Teacher's Pet Publications, Inc.

UNIT OBJECTIVES-*The Great Gilly Hopkins*

1. Through reading Katherine Paterson's *The Great Gilly Hopkins*, students will gain an appreciation for our basic need to belong.

2. Students will determine characters' status as static or dynamic.

3. Students will examine their own and the main character's racial prejudices.

4. Students will be exposed to components and aspects of foster care.

5. Students will gain appreciation for and demonstrate proficiency in identifying and using figurative language.

6. Students will demonstrate their understanding of the text on four levels: factual, interpretive, critical and personal.

7. Students will be given the opportunity to practice both reading aloud and reading silently to improve their skills in each area.

8. Students will answer questions to demonstrate their knowledge and understanding of the main events and characters in *The Great Gilly Hopkins* as they relate to the author's theme development.

9. Students will enrich their vocabularies and improve their understanding of the novel through the vocabulary lessons prepared for use in conjunction with the novel.

10. The writing assignments in this unit are geared to several purposes:
    a. to have students demonstrate their abilities to inform, to persuade, or to express their own personal ideas
       Note: Students will demonstrate the ability to write effectively to <u>inform</u> by developing and organizing facts to convey information. Students will demonstrate the ability to write effectively to <u>persuade</u> by selecting and organizing relevant information, establishing an argumentative purpose, and by designing an appropriate strategy for an identified audience. Students will demonstrate the ability to write effectively to <u>express personal ideas</u> by selecting a form and its appropriate elements.
    b. To check the students' reading comprehension
    c. To make students think about the ideas presented by the novel
    d. To encourage logical thinking

READING ASSIGNMENT SHEET - *The Great Gilly Hopkins*

Date Assigned	Reading Assignment (Chapters)	Completion Date
	Set 1 Welcome to Thompson Park The Man Who Comes to Supper	
	Set 2 More Unpleasant Surprises Sarsaparilla to Sorcery	
	Set 3 William Earnest and Other Mean Flowers Harassing Miss Harris Dust and Desperation	
	Set 4 The One-Way Ticket *Pow*	
	Set 5 The Visitor Never and Other Canceled Promises The Going	
	Set 6 Jackson, Virginia She'll Be Riding Six White Horses (When She Comes) Homecoming	

UNIT OUTLINE - *The Great Gilly Hopkins*

1 Introduction Materials PVR Set 1	2 Study? Set 1 PVR Set 2	3 Study? Set 2 PVR Set 3	4 Study? Set 3 Letter writing	5 Nonfiction Rdg Writing Assignment #1
6 PVR Set 4 Oral Rdg Evaluation	7 Study ? Set 4 Writing Assignment #2 PVR Set 5	8 Figurative Language	9 Study ? Set 5 PVR Set 6	10 Study ? Set 6 Theme & Characterization
11 Writing Assignment #3	12 Nonfiction Discussion Share Writing Assignments	13 Extra Discussion Questions Writing Conference	14 Extra Discussion Questions/ Activities	15 Speaker
16 Vocabulary Review	17 Review	18 Test		

Key: P = Preview Study Questions   V = Vocabulary Work   R = Read

STUDY GUIDE QUESTIONS

SHORT ANSWER STUDY GUIDE QUESTIONS - *The Great Gilly Hopkins*

Set 1
1. Describe Galadriel Hopkins.
2. Who is Miss Ellis?
3. How does Maime Trotter greet her new foster child?
4. Who is William Earnest Teague?
5. Right from the start, what does Gilly do to make herself feel like she is in charge at Trotter's?
6. How does Maime Trotter's house compare to the Nevins' place?
7. What is Gilly's first impression of Trotter?
8. How does Trotter set Gilly straight about W.E. and her swearing?
9. Identify the man who comes to supper.
10. What does Gilly promise herself that she will do at the end of the chapter, "Man Who Comes to Supper"?

Set 2
1. Why is Gilly angry the morning Trotter is to take her to school?
2. What is her reaction to Miss Harris and her new class in Harris -6?
3. Explain what happens on the playground at recess.
4. Describe Agnes Stokes.
5. From whom does Gilly receive a postcard upon returning from day two at school?
6. Why does W.E. move closer to Trotter during dinner?
7. For what reason does Gilly go over to Mr. Randolph's after supper?
8. What does she find as she is trying to straighten up Mr. Randolph's books?
9. Which book does Trotter select for Gilly to read from and why?
10. How is Mr. Randolph affected by the reading?
11. What is Gilly's reaction to the poem?
12. How does W.E. contribute to the discussion of the poem?
13. Explain this chapter's title.
14. What is Gilly planning at the end of chapter four?

Set 3
1. How do Gilly and Agnes get along?
2. When W.E. brings Gilly a tray of Trotter's cookies and milk, what plan does she devise?
3. How do Gilly and William Earnest spend their time after supper?
4. What is Trotter's reaction to this turn of events?
5. How does Gilly try to 'get to' Miss Harris?
6. Does Gilly get the expected response from her teacher? Explain.
7. Why does Gilly find it urgent to try to leave Thompson Park as soon as possible?

(continued on next page)

Short Answer Study Guide Questions - *The Great Gilly Hopkins* Page 2

8. How does Gilly employ W.E. and Agnes in her first plan?
9. What is Gilly's second plan to get into Mr. Randolph's house? Is it successful?
10. Why and to whom does Gilly write at the end of the chapter, "Dust and Desperation"?

Set 4

1. How does Gilly feel about Trotter's church?
2. Why does Trotter send Gilly upstairs after dinner? What does she do?
3. Who asks Gilly not to leave?
4. Why does Gilly hand the ticket back to the bus station clerk?
5. What happens next at the bus station?
6. Where do the police take her and what happens there?
7. Why do Miss Ellis and Trotter argue?
8. How does Trotter handle the issue of the stolen money?
9. What does Gilly teach William Earnest?
10. How does Trotter feel about the lessons?

Set 5

1. Why was Gilly absent the Tuesday and Wednesday before Thanksgiving?
2. Who shows up at Trotter's on Thanksgiving?
3. Describe the scene at Trotter's that day.
4. What does the little lady claiming to be Gilly's grandmother tell her?
5. When do all of them finally eat their Thanksgiving meal?
6. What does Gilly tell Agnes that Agnes says is stupid?
7. Who is waiting at Trotter's when she and W.E. return from school? What news does she bring?
8. Describe the dinner scene that night at Trotter's.
9. What is Mr. Randolph's farewell gift for Gilly?
10. What does Trotter share with Gilly that night when she comforts Gilly from her bad dream?

Set 6

1. How is the car ride from Trotter's to Jackson, Virginia with her grandmother?
2. Which bedroom does Gilly prefer and why?
3. What change takes place with her grandmother that begins to irritate Gilly?
4. Where does Gilly place Courtney's picture?
5. What does Gilly write about in her letters to W.E.?
6. What does Miss Harris send to Gilly and why?
7. How is it going for Gilly in her new school?
8. Whose Christmas visit do Nonnie and Gilly prepare for excitedly?
9. Why is Gilly shocked upon meeting Courtney? Why is Nonnie upset?
10. How does Gilly deal with her fear and disappointment?

STUDY GUIDE QUESTIONS ANSWER KEY - *The Great Gilly Hopkins*

Set 1

1. Describe Galadriel Hopkins.
   She is an eleven-year-old foster child who has been constantly moved around. This is her third placement in three years. She prides herself on being brilliant, clever, and hard to manage. Her nickname is Gruesome Gilly.

2. Who is Miss Ellis?
   Miss Ellis is Gilly's blond- haired, blue- eyed case worker.

3. How does Maime Trotter greet her new foster child?
   Maime claims to never have met a kid she couldn't make friends with. She tells Gilly she belongs there now and calls her Gilly, honey.

4. Who is William Earnest Teague?
   He is Trotter's younger foster boy who has muddy brown hair and thick metal-framed glasses.

5. Right from the start, what does Gilly do to make herself feel like she is in charge at Trotter's ?
   She boldly wipes dust off the piano seat before sitting, makes a scary face at William Earnest, and bangs on the piano as the two women are talking.

6. How does Maime Trotter's house compare to the Nevins' place?
   It is a much smaller, older, and more cluttered home than from where Gilly had just lived with the Nevins in Hollywood Gardens.

7. What is Gilly's first impression of Trotter?
   She thinks she is a hippopotamus of a woman with terrible teeth. She irritates Gilly with her warmth and familiar ways. She calls her a freak.

8. How does Trotter set Gilly straight about W.E. and her swearing?
   She lets Gilly know she will not tolerate taking the Lord's name in vain in her house and that in no way is she to hurt W.E. He is under her protection now, and ain't nobody on earth gonna hurt him.

9. Identify the man who comes to supper.
   Mr. Randolph lives next door to Trotter. He is a little, blind black man.

10. What does Gilly promise herself that she will do at the end of the chapter "Man Who Comes to Supper"?
    She promises herself for the millionth time that she will find out where her mother, Courtney Rutherford Hopkins, lives and write to her to tell her to come and take her beautiful daughter, Galadriel, home.

Set 2

1. Why is Gilly angry the morning Trotter is to take her to school?
   She is upset because Trotter doesn't seem to notice how messy her hair looks and when she goes upstairs to fix it, Trotter asks her to make the beds.

2. What is her reaction to Miss Harris and her new class in Harris -6?
   She is stunned to discover that her teacher is black and that half of the class is black as well. She is mortified to learn that she will begin behind in her skills as compared to them, too.

3. Explain what happens on the playground at recess.
   She snags a loose basketball and she runs with it and shoots to her heart's delight. The boys chase her and tackle her to the ground. There are six of them to one of her. They are all marched to the principal's office by Miss Harris where they are lectured. Mr. Evans detains Gilly and offers her help and reminds her she can make a new start there. He also insists on no fighting at this school anywhere.

4. Describe Agnes Stokes.
   She is another sixth-grader from the other class. She has long, greasy red hair and lives with her grandmother. She wants to be Gilly's friend.

5. From whom does Gilly receive a postcard upon returning from day two at school?
   She receives a postcard postmarked California from Courtney Hopkins, her mother.

6. Why does W.E. move closer to Trotter during dinner?
   Gilly continues to scare him when Trotter isn't looking.

7. For what reason does Gilly go over to Mr. Randolph's after supper?
   Trotter would like Gilly to read to all of them and Mr. Randolph has hundreds of books at his house. The only book available to read at Trotters was the Holy Bible and Gilly did not want to have to read it aloud.

8. What does she find as she is trying to straighten up Mr. Randolph's books?
   Two five dollar bills flutter down from the behind an encyclopedia.

9. Which book does Trotter select for Gilly to read from and why?
   Trotter comes over to help Gilly and chooses *The Oxford Book of English Verse,* one of Mr. Randolph's favorites.

10. How is Mr. Randolph affected by the reading?
    Mr. Randolph becomes engrossed in the reading; reciting along with Gilly's reading in a warm and soft voice.

11. What is Gilly's reaction to the poem?
    She was impressed with the music of its words, but she told Mr. Randolph it was stupid.

12. How does W.E. contribute to the discussion of the poem?
    When Gilly asks Mr. Randolph what Wordsworth meant by 'the meanest flower that blows', W.E. surprisingly responds with the answer, "dandelion."

13. Explain this chapter's title.
    Sorcery to Sarsaparilla is the title of the encyclopedia from which behind the money came fluttering.

14. What is Gilly planning at the end of chapter four?
    She plans to somehow return to Mr. Randolph's to search for more money.

Set 3

1. How do Gilly and Agnes get along?
   Gilly decides she may need Agnes some day, so she tolerates her although she doesn't really care for her. Gilly is very bossy and demands silence from Agnes

2. When W.E. brings Gilly a tray of Trotter's cookies and milk, what plan does she devise?
   She suddenly decides that W.E. may come in handy someday and she entertains herself with possible criminal names for him. Immediately after she finishes her snack, she goes down and watches TV with him.

3. How do Gilly and William Earnest spend their time after supper?
   Gilly makes him a paper airplane and shows him how to fly it. William Earnest is beaming with pride over this accomplishment.

4. What is Trotter's reaction to this turn of events?
   She is thrilled and gives Gilly a look and words of praise that are difficult for Gilly to accept.

5. How does Gilly try to 'get to' Miss Harris?
   She is disturbed by Miss Harris' seeming lack of emotional dependence on her class. She is too impersonal for Gilly and she wants to stir things up. She creates an illustrated poem that is very demeaning in a racial way towards Miss Harris' race. She anonymously places it in Miss Harris math book early in the morning.

6. Does Gilly get the expected response from her teacher? Explain.
   No, she does not. She anxiously awaits a blow-up all day and there never is one. After school, Miss Harris asks Gilly to wait and she talks to her very calmly about them both having a lot of anger. The teacher envies Gilly because Gilly is able to express her anger and Miss Harris represses hers. Gilly is shocked with this unexpected reaction and runs all the way home.

7. Why does Gilly find it urgent to try to leave Thompson Park as soon as possible?
   She is afraid that she is turning soft. This place is messing her up and she needs to stay tough.

8. How does Gilly employ W.E. and Agnes in her first plan?
   Agnes acts as a guard outside Mr. Randolph's house, while Gilly hoists W.E. up so he can look behind the books in the bookcase near where the other money fell out. He discovers a wad of bills and hands them over to Gilly. She leads him to believe it is all a good surprise for Mr. Randolph.

9. What is Gilly's second plan to get into Mr. Randolph's house? Is it successful?
   Gilly masterminds a cleaning scam. She thoroughly cleans Trotter's house and then offers to clean Mr. Randolph's. She gets in to his house and cleans, but does not find any more money.

10. Why and to whom does Gilly write at the end of the chapter, "Dust and Desperation"?
    She writes a letter to her mother asking her to send her the needed money for a bus ticket so she can join her in California. She claims that Trotter is a religious fanatic, William Earnest is retarded, and that she is being mistreated.

Set 4

1. How does Gilly feel about Trotter's church?
   She is very critical of the Sunday School teacher and the minister who uses poor grammar. Trotter is outraged at her comments.

2. Why does Trotter send Gilly upstairs after dinner? What does she do?
   There is a stain on Mr. Randolph's tie and his son will be coming soon. Trotter sends Gilly upstairs to get one of her deceased husband's ties for him. Gilly sees cash lying in Trotter's open purse and takes it. This is all she needs to be able to buy the bus ticket for California. She goes upstairs to pack after Trotter settles on the couch for an afternoon nap.

3. Who asks Gilly not to leave?
   William Earnest begs Gilly to stay. She tells him she has to leave.

4. Why does Gilly hand the ticket back to the bus station clerk?
   She wants to leave sooner than 8:30, so the clerk takes the ticket back to fix her a new ticket that will take her to Washington where she can transfer to a California bus.

5. What happens next at the bus station?
   The police come and take Gilly to the police station.

6. What happens there?
   The police search her suitcase and find Trotter's address on the postcard from Courtney. They call Trotter. She and William Earnest show up to take her home.

7. What did Miss Ellis and Trotter argue about?
   Miss Ellis wants to remove Gilly from Trotter's foster home and Trotter insists that she stay. They put the choice in Gilly's hands and she chooses to stay until her mother comes for her.

8. How does Trotter handle the issue of the stolen money?
   She has Gilly return Mr. Randolph's money to him and then she makes Gilly earn back the remainder of the missing money through various jobs. The highest paying job is helping William Earnest with his homework.

9. What does Gilly teach William Earnest?
   She determines that W.E. needs to be able to defend himself and not hide behind Trotter anymore. She teaches him how to stick up for himself. He practices his newly learned strategy on Trotter.

10. How does Trotter feel about the lessons?
    She is a little uneasy, but Gilly explains that he needs to be able to stand up for himself. She accepts this and says to go ahead. Trotter can't bear to watch Gilly teach W. E. self-defense, which she calls boxing lessons.

Set 5

1. Why was Gilly absent the Tuesday and Wednesday before Thanksgiving?
   Everyone in the house, including Mr. Randolph, were sick with the flu. Gilly was taking care of all of them.

2. Who shows up at Trotter's on Thanksgiving?
   A little old lady with a Southern accent claiming to be Gilly's grandmother appears at their door on Thanksgiving.

3. Describe the scene at Trotter's that day.
   William Earnest cries for Gilly after he wets his bed. Mr. Randolph is sleeping on a cot in the dining room. Trotter is a wreck and falls over, pinning Gilly beneath her. The place is a disaster area.

4. What does the little lady claiming to be Gilly's grandmother tell her?
   She tells Gilly that she was unaware that her daughter had a baby and that she had just heard from Courtney for the first time in thirteen years asking her to check on Gilly. Courtney had received Gilly's letter and was worried about her.

5. When do all of them finally eat their Thanksgiving meal?
   They finally eat their Thanksgiving meal on Saturday evening. Gilly prepared it and everyone flatters her for the job she did. When asked about the earlier visitor, Gilly lies and says it was someone from a church looking for new members.

6. What does Gilly tell Agnes that Agnes says is stupid?
   She tells Agnes she was out of school because her family was ill: her mother, her brother, and her uncle.

7. Who is waiting at Trotter's when she and W.E. return from school? What news does she bring?
   Miss Ellis brings the news that Gilly's mother wants her to go to live with her grandmother in Virginia. She has spoken with Courtney on the telephone.

8. Describe the dinner scene that night at Trotter's.
   Trotter fixes a grand dinner of her special fried chicken. W.E. is crying openly and the rest of them are very quiet and sad thinking of Gilly's next day departure.

9. What is Mr. Randolph's farewell gift for Gilly?
   He gives her his cherished poetry book from which she read the Wordsworth poem when she first came to Trotter's.

10. What does Trotter share with Gilly that night when she comforts Gilly from her bad dream?
    She tells Gilly that Gilly's leaving is killing her, even though she isn't supposed to let her know how she feels. She tells Gilly to make her proud.

Set 6
1. How is the car ride from Trotter's to Jackson, Virginia with her grandmother?
   Gilly is nervous and wishes her grandmother would turn the ten-year-old station wagon around and take her back to Trotter's.

2. Which bedroom does Gilly prefer and why?
   Nonnie shows her Courtney's room but it is too prissy for Gilly and she allows her to choose another. She chooses Courtney's brother's room. She learns that Chadwell died in Vietnam.

3. What change takes place with her grandmother that begins to irritate Gilly?
   It seems like her grandmother chatters unendingly since she brought Gilly there to her home.

4. Where does Gilly place Courtney's picture?
   She gets it out to place on the dresser and then puts it away again because she doesn't feel like it fits here any better than it fit anywhere else.

5. What does Gilly write about in her letters to W.E.?
   She leads W.E. to believe she is very rich and has horses. She also encourages him to read to Mr. Randolph.

6. What does Miss Harris send to Gilly and why?
   She sends Gilly books written by J.R. Tolkein. She had meant to lend them to her when she was still at Thompson Park, but since Gilly had to leave she sends them as a remembrance of their time together.

7. How is it going for Gilly in her new school?
   Gilly is doing okay. She is mostly impressed with how gutsy her grandmother was when she enrolled her in Jackson Elementary School.

8. Whose Christmas visit do Nonnie and Gilly prepare for excitedly?
   Courtney has called her mother informing her that she will fly in from California on December 23.

9. Why is Gilly shocked upon meeting Courtney? Why is Nonnie upset?
   She doesn't look at all like the picture Gilly has treasured for so long. She only has enough clothes for a two day visit. It is revealed that Nonnie has sent her the money to return.

10. How does Gilly deal with her fear and disappointment?
    She excuses herself to the bathroom and tries to throw up. When that is unsuccessful, she dials Trotter's number and begs to come home. Trotter gives her the strength and encouragement to go out and meet with her mother and grandmother and go home with them.

MULTIPLE CHOICE STUDY GUIDE / QUIZ QUESTIONS- *The Great Gilly Hopkins*

Set 1

1. Galadriel Hopkins is
   a. a foster child.
   b. an eleven-year old girl.
   c. brilliant, clever, and hard to manage.
   d. all of the above

2. Miss Ellis is
   a. Gilly's teacher from Hollywood Gardens.
   b. Gilly's case worker.
   c. Gilly's long lost aunt from California.
   d. Gilly's new foster mother.

3. Maime Trotter says she never met a kid she couldn't make friends with.
   a. true
   b. false

4. William Earnest Teague is
   a. Gilly's new foster brother.
   b. author of Gilly's favorite book.
   c. Maime Trotter's next door neighbor.
   d. none of the above

5. Gilly starts out with Maime Trotter by
   a. being sweet and polite when talked to by anyone.
   b. holding the door open for Miss Ellis and her.
   c. acting rude and banging on the piano.
   d. all of the above

6. Compared to the Nevins' house in Hollywood Gardens Maime Trotter's house is
   a. cleaner
   b. dirtier
   c. smaller
   d. both b and c

7. Gilly thinks Maime Trotter is a friendly, warm soul at first.
   a. true
   b. false

Gilly Multiple Choice Study/Quiz Questions Page 2

8. What two things does Trotter set Gilly straight on right from the start?
    a. her swearing
    b. hurting William Earnest
    c. cleaning detail
    d. both a and b
    e. both a and c

9. The man who comes to supper is
    a. Maime's neighbor, Mr. Randolph.
    b. Maime's son who lives across town.
    c. Gilly's case worker, Mr. Rudolph.
    d. the minister at Maime's Baptist church.

10. At the end of the second chapter, Gilly promises herself she will
    a. run away as soon as she has enough money.
    b. write to her aunt to come and get her.
    c. find her mother, Courtney Hopkins.
    d. start a new life here in Thompson Park.

Gilly Multiple Choice Study/Quiz Questions Page 3

Set 2

1. Gilly is angry the morning Trotter is to take her to school because
   a. she thinks Trotter is a religious fanatic.
   b. she doesn't think Trotter cares how she looks for her first day at school.
   c. Trotter asks her to make the beds while she is upstairs.
   d. Both b and c

2. Gilly is excited to have an intelligent teacher and be placed in the challenging sixth grade at Thompson Park.
   a. true
   b. false

3. During recess on her first day at Thompson Park, Gilly
   a. asks the teacher on duty if she can help her.
   b. steals a basketball from some boys and gets in a fight.
   c. calls some black kids bad names.
   d. makes three new friends.

4. Agnes Stokes is
   a. the only other white girl that is in Gilly's class.
   b. a popular girl from Gilly's class.
   c. a red-haired girl from the other sixth grade class.
   d. Gilly's friend form Hollywood Gardens.

5. Gilly receives a postcard postmarked San Francisco, California from
   a. Courtney Rutherford Hopkins.
   b. the Rice A Roni Company sending a free coupon.
   c. her father, whom she finally located.
   d. Alcatraz prison, a place she had written requesting some information.

6. Why does William Earnest move closer to Trotter during supper?
   a. He misses Trotter after being at school all day long.
   b. He can't see well enough to eat alone.
   c. He wants to be near so he can help Mr. Randolph with his napkin and silverware.
   d. He is afraid of Gilly's mean faces and strange actions.

Gilly Multiple Choice Study/Quiz Questions Page 4

7. Gilly is sent to Mr. Randolph's after supper to
    a. locate something to read other than Maime's Bible.
    b. try to find the stepladder to clean the chandelier.
    c. clean up his house for him.
    d. none of the above

8. What surprise is Gilly in for when she goes to Mr. Randolph's?
    a. He has a pet monkey that she likes to play with over there.
    b. He has hundreds of books from which to choose.
    c. Two five dollar bills flutter down from behind an encyclopedia on the bookshelf.
    d. William Earnest ran over to Mr. Randolph's and scares her as she enters the house

9. Trotter comes over to help Gilly and selects
    a. another version other than The Saint James version of the Bible.
    b. *The Oxford Book of English Verse*
    c. some magazines of Mr. Randolph's.
    d. a favorite mystery book of Mr. Randolph's.

10. When Gilly starts reading the Wordsworth poem, Mr. Randolph
    a. can't remember which poem it is that he used to love so dearly.
    b. gets up and walks slowly around the room to the rhthym of the words.
    c. breaks down into tears.
    d. recites it along with her reading it in a soft and warm voice.

11. When asked for her opinion of the poem she just read, Gilly says it is
    a. beautiful.
    b. stupid.
    c. too long.
    d. boring.

12. What part of the poem does William Earnest understand?
    a. the part about the meanest flower.
    b. the part about the trailing clouds of glory.
    c. the part about death and birth.
    d. none of the above

Gilly Multiple Choice Study/Quiz Questions Page 5

13. The title to chapter four refers to
    a. two of Gilly's spelling list words.
    b. two of Gilly's favorite things.
    c. the title of the encyclopedia from which the money fell.
    d. some words that Gilly needed to look up in the encyclopedia.

14. Gilly plans to return to Mr. Randolph's to search for more money soon.
    a. true
    b. false

Gilly Multiple Choice Study/Quiz Questions Page 6

Set 3

1. Gilly and Agnes have become best friends.
    a. true
    b. false

2. When W.E. brings Gilly a tray of milk and cookies, she
    a. thanks him nicely and shuts the door behind him.
    b. scares him by jumping out from under the bed.
    c. slams the door in his face.
    d. devises a plan to win him over for her own good.

3. After supper, Gilly and William Earnest
    a. fly a paper airplane that Gilly made for William Earnest.
    b. go outside to play with their new jar of bubbles.
    c. both help Trotter with the dishes and then walk Mr. Randolph home.
    d. watch Sesame Street together in the living room.

4. Gilly is comfortable with Trotter's praise and kindness.
    a. true
    b. false

5. Gilly decides she must stir Miss Harris up by
    a. putting a whoopie cushion on her seat before she sits down.
    b. refusing to turn in her homework.
    c. creating a card with racial slurs and anonymously leaving it for her.
    d. letting the air out of her tires.

6. Miss Harris responds just like all the other teachers Gilly harassed.
    a. true
    b. false

7. After the incident with Miss Harris, Gilly decides
    a. she's got to get out of Thompson Park as soon as possible before she turns soft.
    b. to get back at Miss Harris again in some other way.
    c. she'll play a trick on Trotter too.
    d. to get back at the principal too.

Gilly Multiple Choice Study/Quiz Questions Page 7

8. How does Gilly use William Earnest and Agnes in her next plan?
   a. Agnes is to put the new card on Miss Harris' desk while she takes W.E. to his room.
   b. Agnes is to distract W.E. while Gilly does what she needs to do.
   c. William Earnest hides the money while Agnes looks for more.
   d. Agnes stands guard while W.E. looks for the money.

9. How does Gilly manage to get back in Mr. Randolph's house again with him there?
   a. She sneaks in when he is sleeping.
   b. She comes to get him for supper and waits while he washes up before leaving.
   c. She offers to clean his house for him and since he is blind he can't see what she is up to.
   d. She comes over to borrow the stepladder to clean Trotter's chandelier.

10. Who does Gilly write to at the end of "Dust and Desperation"?
    a. her mother, Courtney Hopkins.
    b. Miss Ellis, her case worker.
    c. the minister at the church.
    d. Mrs. Nevins, her last foster mother.

Gilly Multiple Choice Study/Quiz Questions Page 8

Set 4

1. When Gilly voices her opinion about the minister to Trotter
   a. Trotter says she is thinking of going to the black Baptist church with Mr. Randolph.
   b. Trotter explodes and says," who am I to pass judgment on the Lord's anointed?"
   c. William Earnest agrees with Gilly so Trotter wants to find a better church for them.
   d. Trotter very patiently explains that he is new and hasn't learned the ways yet.

2. What does Gilly do when she is sent upstairs to Trotter's room?
   a. She gets a gaudy tie of Melvin's for Mr. Randolph.
   b. She steals money out of Maime's open purse.
   c. She makes the beds that are unmade.
   d. Both a and b

3. What does Gilly do when Trotter is finally asleep on the couch?
   a. She runs upstairs to pack her suitcase.
   b. She tells William Earnest she has to go.
   c. She leaves the house and runs down the hill.
   d. All of the above.

4. Why doesn't Gilly take the first ticket the bus station clerk issues?
   a. It doesn't leave for four hours and she wants to get going sooner.
   b. She wants to go to Washington D.C. first.
   c. She can't decide what to do next.
   d. She gets too nervous and makes a mistake.

5. The police come to the bus station and take Gilly away with them.
   a. true
   b. false

6. The last thing that happens at the police station is
   a. Miss Ellis shows up to take Gilly to Social Services.
   b. The police search through Gilly's suitcase.
   c. Trotter and William Earnest come in a taxi to take Gilly home.
   d. Mr. Randolph calls the police station wondering where his neighbors have gone.

Gilly Multiple Choice Study/Quiz Questions Page 9

7. When Gilly comes home from school the next day she overhears
    a. Miss Ellis and Trotter arguing.
    b. William Earnest crying because he has to leave Trotter.
    c. a phone call from someone in Virginia.
    d. Trotter say that she just can't keep Gilly any longer after she has stolen from her.

8. How does Trotter manage Gilly's debt?
    a. She has her ask Mr. Randolph for a loan.
    b. She lists the rates by which Gilly can earn back the missing money.
    c. She signs Gilly up at the church for community service.
    d. She has Gilly write an apology to Mr. Randolph and to her.

9. What does Gilly teach William Earnest?
    a. Gilly teaches William Earnest how to play basketball.
    b. She helps him do origami.
    c. She tells him the ways to drive a teacher wild.
    d. Gilly teaches W.E. how to stand up for himself.

10. When Trotter finds out what Gilly is teaching William Earnest she
    a. is proud.
    b. is worried.
    c. can't watch.
    d. all of the above

Gilly Multiple Choice Study/Quiz Questions Page 10

Set 5

1. Gilly missed the Tuesday and Wednesday before Thanksgiving because
   a. everyone in her household was ill with the flu.
   b. she didn't understand her math problems.
   c. Agnes was beginning to get on her nerves.
   d. she was embarrassed about her card to Miss Harris.

2. The visitor who shows up at Trotter's on Thanksgiving Day is
   a. Gilly's mother, Courtney.
   b. Gilly's grandmother, Courtney's mother.
   c. Miss Harris inquiring about Gilly's absences.
   d. none of the above

3. Select the one thing that did not happen at Trotters on Thanksgiving Day.
   a. An uninvited visitor shows up at the door.
   b. Mr. Randolph's son came looking for him.
   c. William Earnest wet his pants and bed.
   d. Trotter fell on Gilly and squashed her.

4. Mrs. Hopkins tells Gilly that she did not know that she had a grandchild.
   a. true
   b. false

5. When did Trotter's family finally eat their Thanksgiving meal?
   a. Sunday night they were all feeling better and ate a great meal.
   b. Friday night Trotter had enough energy to finally cook the turkey.
   c. They had to throw the turkey out because it rotted.
   d. none of the above

6. Agnes told Gilly that when she called Trotter, her mother, and William Earnest, her brother, it sounded sweet.
   a. true
   b. false

7. What news does Miss Ellis bring to Trotter's the Monday after Thanksgiving.
   a. Courtney has called her from California.
   b. Courtney wants Gilly to live with her grandmother in Virginia.
   c. Both a and b
   d. None of the above

Gilly Multiple Choice Study/Quiz Questions Page 11

8. Describe the scene at Trotter's that evening for supper.
   a. William Earnest was crying during dinner.
   b. Maime had made fried chicken.
   c. Nobody had much to say because they were all in shock.
   d. All of the above

9. What does Mr. Randolph give Gilly for a farewell gift?
   a. He gives her the money she repaid him.
   b. He promises he will come to see her when his son from Virginia gets him.
   c. He gives her the poetry book from which she read the Wordsworth poem.
   d. He gives her the encyclopedia that hid the two five dollar bills.

10. What does Trotter share with Gilly that night when she comforts Gilly from her bad dream?
    a. She tells Gilly that Gilly's leaving is killing her
    b. She tells Gilly to make her proud.
    c. She tells Gilly that she will come and see her right away to be sure she is OK.
    d. Both a and b

Gilly Multiple Choice Study/Quiz Questions Page 12

Set 6

1. Galadriel tells Mrs. Hopkins to turn her ten-year-old station wagon around and take her back to Trotters.
   a. true
   b. false

2. Which bedroom does Gilly choose to stay in at her grandmother's?
   a. Courtney's
   b. Chadwell's
   c. the guest room

3. How does her grandmother change after Gilly arrives?
   a. She wants Gilly to call her granny.
   b. She asks Gilly to wear Courtney's old clothes.
   c. She starts talking nonstop.
   d. She wants Gilly to have tea parties everyday at noon.

4. Gilly asks her Grandmother for
   a. a frame for Courtney's picture.
   b. some baby and childhood pictures of Courtney.
   c. a new coat for the cold weather.
   d. none of the above

5. Gilly writes to William Earnest about
   a. the horses they own and how she takes care of them.
   b. how rich they are in Virginia.
   c. both a and b
   d. her new school and teachers.

6. Miss Harris, Gilly's teacher from Thompson Park, sends Gilly
   a. the poem she wrote for her.
   b. a set of books by J.R. Tolkein.
   c. a picture of herself that resembled the cut-out magazine picture on the poem.
   d. a long letter telling Gilly about her anger.

Gilly Multiple Choice Study/Quiz Questions Page 13

7. When Nonnie takes Galadriel to Jackson Elementary she
   a. breaks down in front of the principal.
   b. buys her new clothes for the occasion.
   c. answers the principal's questions without the blink of an eye.
   d. both b and c

8. To prepare for Courtney's visit Nonnie and Gilly
   a. put up and trim a tall Christmas tree.
   b. have their hair done.
   c. invite their neighbors in for tea.
   d. both a and b

9. Why is Gilly stunned and upset at the airport?
   a. Courtney looks nothing like her picture.
   b. Nonnie sent Courtney the money to fly home to see her.
   c. Courtney only plans to stay for two days.
   d. All of the above

10. How does Gilly deal with her fear and disappointment?
    a. She excuses herself to the bathroom and tries to throw up.
    b. She dials Trotter's number and begs her to let her to come home.
    c. She runs off as Courtney and Nonnie stand there watching her.
    d. Both a and b

ANSWER KEY- MULTIPLE CHOICE STUDY/QUIZ QUESTIONS
The Great Gilly Hopkins

Set 1	Set 2	Set 3
1. D	1. D	1. B
2. B	2. B	2. D
3. A	3. B	3. A
4. A	4. C	4. B
5. C	5. A	5. C
6. D	6. D	6. B
7. B	7. A	7. A
8. D	8. C	8. D
9. A	9. B	9. C
10. C	10. D	10. A
	11. B	
	12. A	
	13. C	
	14. A	

Set 4	Set 5	Set 6
1. B	1. A	1. B
2. D	2. B	2. B
3. D	3. B	3. C
4. A	4. A	4. D
5. A	5. D	5. C
6. C	6. B	6. B
7. A	7. C	7. D
8. B	8. D	8. D
9. D	9. C	9. D
10. D	10. D	10. D

PREREADING VOCABULARY WORKSHEETS

Vocabulary - *The Great Gilly Hopkins* -Set 1

Welcome to Thompson Park, The Man Who Comes to Supper

Part I: Using Prior Knowledge and Contextual Clues
Below are the sentences in which the vocabulary words appear in the text. Read the sentence. Use any clues you can find in the sentence combined with your prior knowledge, and write what you think the underlined words mean in the space provided.

1. She sat back and tried to chew the bit she had managed to *salvage*.

2. She fished another ball of gum from her jeans pocket and scraped the lint off with her thumbnail before *elaborately* popping it into her mouth.

3. Gilly *obligingly* took the gum out of her mouth while Miss Ellis's eyes were still in the mirror.

4. She gave little W.E. the most fearful face in all her *repertory* of scary looks, sort of a cross between Count Dracula and Godzilla.

5. Gilly favored Miss Ellis with her best *barracuda* smile.

6. ,7. Meantime Trotter was *laboriously* *hefting* herself to her feet.

8. "You just said"- the fat woman's voice was rising, and her knife was crashing down on the carrots with *vengeance*-"you just said William Earnest was"- her voice dropped to a whisper- "retarded."

9., 10. Perhaps the *self-righteous* Trotter would be put in jail for contributing to the *delinquency* of a minor.

Vocabulary - *The Great Gilly Hopkins* Set 1 continued

Part II: Determining the Meaning Match the vocabulary words to their dictionary definitions.

____ 1. salvage   A. in an obeying manner
____ 2. elaborately   B. neglect; wrongdoing
____ 3. obligingly   C. with great difficulty
____ 4. repertory   D. predatory fish
____ 5. barracuda   E. pure
____ 6. laboriously   F. collection
____ 7. hefting   G. rescue; save
____ 8. vengeance   H. revenge
____ 9. self-righteous I. lifting
____10. delinquency   J. with great detail

Vocabulary - *The Great Gilly Hopkins* Set 2

More Unpleasant Surprises, Sarsaparilla to Sorcery

Part I: Below are the sentences in which the vocabulary words appear in the text. Read the sentence. Use any clues you can find in the sentence combined with your prior knowledge, and write what you think the underlined words mean in the space provided.

1. Trotter missed the look, but not Gilly, who smiled widely and shook her half-bulldozed head *emphatically*.

2. She would read on and on forever, while the two of them nodded *piously* at each other.

3. She spit every *obscenity* she'd ever heard through her teeth, but it wasn't enough.

4. That walrus-faced *imbecile*!

5. When despite her assault by comb and scissors a few strands refused to lie down meekly, she soaked them mercilessly into *submission*.

6. She'd show them who Galadriel Hopkins was- she was not to be *trifled* with.

7. "Well, Gilly's a fine name," said Mr. Evans, which *confirmed* to Gilly that at school, too, she was fated to be surrounded by fools.

8. Gilly shook her head. Inside she *seethed*.

9. She'd actually drawn blood in the *fracas*.

10. To Gilly's relief, the blind man's attention was *diverted* from his tale of childhood schooldays to the organization of the food on his plate,

Vocabulary - *The Great Gilly Hopkins* Set 2 continued

Part II: Determining the Meaning Match the vocabulary words to their dictionary definitions.

___ 11. emphatically   A. dimwit; moron
___ 12. piously   B. toyed or played with
___ 13. obscenity   C. proved
___ 14. imbecile   D. uproar
___ 15. submission   E. changed; distracted
___ 16. trifled   F. intensely
___ 17. confirmed   G. meekness; surrender
___ 18. seethed   H. swearing
___ 19. fracas   I. raged; fumed
___ 20. diverted   J. in a holy manner

Vocabulary - *The Great Gilly Hopkins* - Set 3

William Earnest and Other Mean Flowers, Harassing Miss Harris, Dust and Desperation

Part I: Using Prior Knowledge and Contextual Clues
Below are the sentences in which the vocabulary words appear in the text. Read the sentence. Use any clues you can find in the sentence combined with your prior knowledge, and write what you think the underlined words mean in the space provided.

1. Agnes tilted backward to get her face out of Gilly's *leering* one.

2. Gilly smiled *benignly*. "We'll see," she said.

3. The possibilities were unlimited and *delectable*.

4. She slid down beside him, and when his eyes checked her out sideways, she gave a quiet, sisterly kind of smile and pretended to be *enthralled* with Big Bird.

5. "I say"- the veins on his neck stuck out with the effort of raising his voice to an *audible* level- "I say, It sure fly good."

6. Of course, no one knew that he knew, so an army of school *psychologists* had been called in to try to figure her out.

7. Cursing her *incompetence*, she stole one of Trotter's magazines and cut from it a picture of a tall, beautiful black woman in an Afro.

8. Her only regret was that the card was to be *anonymous*.

9. By supper the next night she had finished cleaning everything except the living room *chandelier*.

10. The foster mother is a religious *fanatic*.

Vocabulary - *The Great Gilly Hopkins* Set 3 continued

Part II: Determining the Meaning Match the vocabulary words to their dictionary definitions.

___ 21. leering A. favorably
___ 23. benignly B. inability; failing
___ 22. delectable C. fascinated
___ 24. enthralled D. maniac
___ 25. audible E. glass light hanging from ceiling
___ 26. psychologists F. unsigned
___ 27. incompetence G. glaring
___ 28. anonymous H. hearable
___ 29. chandelier I. delicious
___ 30. fanatic J. therapists

Vocabulary - *The Great Gilly Hopkins* - Set 4

The One-Way Ticket, *Pow*

Part I: Using Prior Knowledge and Contextual Clues
Below are the sentences in which the vocabulary words appear in the text. Read the sentence. Use any clues you can find in the sentence combined with your prior knowledge, and write what you think the underlined words mean in the space provided.

1. "Who am I," she thundered, "to pass judgment on the Lord's *anointed*?"

2. The Sunday after the *futile* dusting Mr. Randolph surprised everyone by refusing seconds.

3. But it was not that silly little *flirtation* that was bothering her.

4. She chose the *gaudiest* one there.

5. The blond policeman *riffled* carelessly through her clothes.

6. Gilly's whole body was *engulfed* in a great aching.

7. W.E. wasn't a *fluted* antique cup in Mrs. Nevin's china cupboard.

8. , 9. "*Pow?*" he echoed softly, *tentatively* doubling up his fist and giving a *feeble* swing.

10. She looked up into the fat, *stricken* face.

Vocabulary - *The Great Gilly Hopkins* Set 4 continued

Part II: Determining the Meaning Match the vocabulary words to their dictionary definitions.

___ 31. anointed   A. useless
___ 32. futile   B. flashiest
___ 33. flirtation   C. flooded
___ 34. gaudiest   D. dedicated
___ 35. riffled   E. weak
___ 36. engulfed   F. having grooves
___ 37. fluted   G. searched
___ 38. tentatively H. with uncertainty
___ 39. feeble   I. teasing
___ 40. stricken   J. troubled

Vocabulary - *The Great Gilly Hopkins* - Set 5

Visitor, Never and Other Canceled Promises, Going

Part I: Using Prior Knowledge and Contextual Clues
Below are the sentences in which the vocabulary words appear in the text. Read the sentence. Use any clues you can find in the sentence combined with your prior knowledge, and write what you think the underlined words mean in the space provided.

1. Trotter recognized this *appalling* possibility, but maintained that there was some moral obligation to inform next of kin when one took to one's bed.

2. It occurred to her that if she could get sick, too, no one would blame her for collapsing, but, of course, she didn't catch anything, except *irritability* from not sleeping properly and worrying.

3. The turkey Trotter had bought was *relentlessly* defrosting on the refrigerator shelf.

4. She had always been-existing from before time-like a goddess in *perpetual* perfection.

5. Both of them sat stark still and listened as it drew *inexorably* nearer.

6. Swaying in the doorway was a huge barefoot *apparition* in striped men's pajamas, gray hair cascading over its shoulders, a wild look in its eyes.

7. "Nobody else." She looked *belligerently* at Trotter, but Trotter was so busy making the meat platter and the salad bowl switch places that the expression was wasted.

8. Alas, Agnes, the world is *woefully* short on frog smoochers.

9. It was the sounds she loved-the sounds that turned and fell in *kaleidoscopic* wonder.

Vocabulary - *The Great Gilly Hopkins* Set 5 continued

10. "I declare, Miss Gilly, you are the only person I know who can rival Mrs. Trotter's *culinary* skill."

Part II: Determining the Meaning   Match the vocabulary words to their dictionary definitions.

___ 41. appalling   A. ghost
___ 42. irritability   B. steadily
___ 43. relentlessly   C. unable to be stopped
___ 44. perpetual   D. shocking
___ 45. inexorably   E. endless
___ 46. apparition   F. testiness
___ 47. belligerently   G. cooking; kitchen
___ 48. woefully   H. brilliant
___ 49. kaleidoscopic   I. with hostility
___ 50. culinary   J. sadly

Vocabulary - *The Great Gilly Hopkins* - Set 6

Jackson, Virginia, She'll Be Riding Six White Horses (When She Comes), Homecoming

Part I: Using Prior Knowledge and Contextual Clues
Below are the sentences in which the vocabulary words appear in the text. Read the sentence. Use any clues you can find in the sentence combined with your prior knowledge, and write what you think the underlined words mean in the space provided.

1. Everything was pink with a four-poster *canopied* bed complete with stuffed animals and dolls.

2. They ate lunch in the dining room with real *monogrammed* silver off silver-rimmed china set on lace mats.

3. In the quiet of Chadwell's room, Gill lay back and gazed out the window at the blue *expanse* of sky.

4. She dulled the *agony* somewhat by plunging into housecleaning for Nonnie.

5. It was a scene that was to repeat itself with *variations* many times in those first couple of weeks.

6. She didn't want to cry in the stupid airport, but just at that moment she heard Nonnie say in a *quavering* voice, "Courtney."

7. Grandparents *laden* with shopping bags of Christmas presents. But no Courtney.

8., 9. Nonnie had sort of put her hand on the younger woman's arm in a timid *embrace*, but there was a huge *embroidered* shoulder bag between the two of them.

10. For a second, the smile, the one *engraved* on Gilly's soul, flashed out.

Vocabulary - *The Great Gilly Hopkins* Set 6 continued

Part II: Determining the Meaning
Match the vocabulary words to their dictionary definitions. If there are words for which you cannot figure out the definition by contextual clues and by process of elimination, look them up in a dictionary.

___ 51. canopied
___ 52. monogrammed
___ 53. expanse
___ 54. agony
___ 55. variations
___ 56. quavering
___ 57. laden
___ 58. embrace
___ 59. embroidered
___ 60. engraved

A. loaded down
B. stretch
C. decoratively covered between bedposts
D. designed with letters
E. trembling
F. hug
G. misery
H. impressed deeply
I. varieties
J. item having needlework

ANSWER KEY - VOCABULARY
The Great Gilly Hopkins

Set 1	Set 2	Set 3
1. G	11. F	21. G
2. J	12. J	22. A
3. A	13. H	23. I
4. F	14. A	24. C
5. D	15. G	25. H
6. C	16. B	26. J
7. I	17. C	27. B
8. H	18. I	28. F
9. E	19. D	29. E
10. B	20. E	30. D

Set 4	Set 5	Set 6
31. D	41. D	51. C
32. A	42. F	52. D
33. I	43. B	53. B
34. B	44. E	54. G
35. G	45. C	55. I
36. C	46. A	56. E
37. F	47. I	57. A
38. H	48. J	58. F
39. E	49. H	59. J
40. J	50. G	60. H

DAILY LESSONS

LESSON ONE

Objectives
1. To introduce *The Great Gilly Hopkins* unit
2. To give students some background information on *The Great Gilly Hopkins*
3. To distribute books and other related materials: study guides, reading assignments
4. To model effective oral reading skills by reading aloud
5. To have students identify point of view

Activity #1
Ask students what they know about foster care and/or foster homes. Examine reasons a child would be placed in foster care. Do they see this type of placement as positive or negative. Have them explain their answers. Ask them if anyone they know has experienced this kind of situation and what were the results? Do they see foster care as a temporary situation or a permanent one? Why? Tell students that in the book they'll be reading, a young girl close to their age, is placed in a foster home for reasons completely out of her control.

Activity #2
Distribute the materials students will use in this unit. Explain in detail how students are to use these materials.

Study Guides
Students should preview the study guide questions before each reading assignment to get a feeling for what events and ideas are important in that section. After reading the section, students will (as a class or individually) answer the questions to review the important events and ideas from that section of the book. Students should keep the study guides as study materials for the unit test.

Vocabulary
Prior to reading an assignment, students will do vocabulary work related to the section of the book they are about to read. Following the completion of the reading of the book, there will be a vocabulary review of all the words used in the vocabulary assignments. Students should keep their vocabulary work as study materials for the unit test.

Reading Assignment Sheet
You need to fill in the reading assignment sheet to let students know when their reading has to be completed. You can either write the assignment sheet on a side blackboard or bulletin board and leave it there for students to see each day, or you can make copies for each student to have. In either case, you should advise students to become very familiar with the reading assignments so they know what is expected of them.

Extra Activities Center

The Unit Resource portion of this unit contains suggestions for a library of related books and articles in your classroom as well as crossword and word search puzzles. Make an extra activities center in your room where you will keep these materials for students to use. (Bring the books and articles in from the library and keep several copies of the puzzles on hand.) Explain to students that these materials are available for students to use when they finish reading assignments or other class work early

Books

Each school has its own rules and regulations regarding student use of school books. Advise students of the procedures that are normal for your school.

Activity #3

Have students examine the cover of the book and turn to page 1. Read pages 1-6 (first chapter) aloud to them as they follow along. Identify the use of third person narration. Encourage students to close their eyes and try to visualize Miss Ellis, Gilly, Maime Trotter, and William Earnest as the author describes them. Discuss the reason Gilly is placed in foster care and the class' reaction to it. Have students recognize the author's frequent stating of Gilly's thoughts, as if they were spoken words. Assign P, V, R for the next chapter.

LESSON TWO

Objectives
1. To review the main ideas and vocabulary from Set 1
2. To preview study questions and vocabulary from Set 2

Activity #1
Review the vocabulary from Set 1 by reproducing the matching section on the chalkboard or on an overhead transparency. Have students volunteer to come up and find the correct match for each vocabulary word. After they have made the match, ask them to use the word in an original sentence. Also have them identify its part of speech.

Activity #2
Discuss the answers to the study questions for these chapters in detail. Write the answers on the board or overhead transparency so students can have the correct answers for study purposes. Note: It is a good practice in public speaking and leadership skills for individual students to take charge of leading the discussions of the study questions. Perhaps a different student could go to the front of the class and lead the discussion each day that the study questions are discussed during this unit. Of course, the teacher should guide the discussion when appropriate and be sure to fill in any gaps the students leave.

Activity #3
Give students the remaining class time to preview the study questions for Set 2 and to do the related vocabulary work. If time allows, begin reading Set 2 or assign the reading of it to be completed prior to the next class session.

LESSON THREE

Objectives
1. To review the vocabulary and main events from Set 2
2. To preview study questions and prereading vocabulary work for Set 3

Activity #1
Review the vocabulary from Set 2 by asking students to practice using the vocabulary in sentences of their own with a partner. After the practice, use the matching section of the prereading vocabulary sheet for Set 2 as a quiz.

Activity #2
Make a copy of the Set 2 study guide questions with answers and the matching vocabulary section. Cut them apart, separating the questions and answers or vocabulary word and definition into two piles. Divide the class into two teams. Give one team the questions (or vocabulary word); the other team the answers (or definition). Divide them up among the players so only one person has one question or answer. Select one team to begin play. One person from that team reads one of the questions or answers. Next, a member from the other team tries to match up with the corresponding response. When it is a correct match, move on to another question. Continue play until all questions are answered correctly.

Activity #3
Give students the remaining class time to preview the study questions for Set 3 and to do the related vocabulary work. If time allows, begin reading Set 3 or assign the reading of it to be completed prior to the next class session

LESSON FOUR

Objectives
1. To review the main events and vocabulary from Set 3
2. To make predictions
3. To give students the opportunity to practice friendly letter writing

Activity #1
Review the vocabulary from Set 3 by dividing the class into small groups. Have students quickly copy the vocabulary words onto blank cards. Next, have them copy the definitions onto separate cards. Turn all the cards over, after mixing them up. Have students take turns flipping two cards over to determine if they are a match. If they are a match, that person gets to keep that pair and gets another turn. Students may look at the vocabulary words in their contextual sentences for help, if needed. Continue play until all words are matched with their definitions. If they are ready for a further challenge, add vocabulary from previous chapters. This is similar to the game Concentration.

Activity #2
Use the multiple choice format of the study guide questions for Set 3 as a quiz to check that students have done the required reading and to review the main ideas of Set 3. Exchange papers for checking and discuss answers.

Activity #3
Discuss the term "prediction". Practice making some simple ones: like the next day's weather or what a classmate will wear the next day. Ask students to get out a piece of paper. Have students make a prediction about what they think will happen in Set 4 of their novels. Have them put these away in a retrievable spot for future review.

Activity #4
Review the letter Gilly writes Courtney on pages 76-77. Compare her letter's form to a standard friendly letter form. Is her letter in correct form? Have students draft friendly letters and address envelopes to someone they choose.

LESSON FIVE

Objectives:
1. To give students practice in writing to inform
2. To give students the opportunity to fulfill the nonfiction reading assignment that goes along with this unit

Activity #1

Allow each of your students to select a topic of interest to them related to racial discrimination or prejudice. Some topics may require a pair of students, or a small group to research. Distribute Writing Assignment #1. Discuss the directions in detail. Take your students to the library so they may work on the assignment. Students should fill out a "Nonfiction Assignment Sheet" for at least one of the sources they used. Students should save these sheets to turn in after lesson twelve when they will share them with the class.

WRITING ASSIGNMENT #1 - *The Great Gilly Hopkins*

PROMPT
You are reading a story in which the main character, a young girl named Gilly, has limited experiences with anyone of a different race. She expresses her biases and judgments through her thoughts, feelings, and actions. At one point, she actually harasses her black sixth grade teacher. Her behaviors are not rational, but based upon fear and suspicion of the unknown and unfamiliar.

Your assignment is to do research on racial prejudice and discrimination. Discover what this bigotry is and how it can be ended. After you have adequate information about this topic, compose a poem that expresses a positive outlook on ending this intolerance.

PREWRITING
You will go to the library. When you get there, use the library's resources to find information about your topic. Look for books, encyclopedias, articles in magazines; anything that will give you the information you require. After you have gathered information and become well-read on the subject, make an outline, and arrange your facts in some order. Make another list of words that express what feelings or reactions the information evoked in you.

DRAFTING
Draw from your list and/or web, combining words, phrases, thoughts, or ideas to write a poem about this subject with a possible resolution of this intolerance. You may use any form of poetry ranging from an acrostic to couplets. Review your English book for some other forms.

PROMPT
When you finish the rough draft of your poem, ask a student who sits near you to read it. After reading your rough draft, he or she should tell you what he or she liked best about your work, which parts were difficult to understand, and ways in which your work could be improved. Reread your poem considering your critic's comments, and make the corrections you think are necessary.

PROOFREADING
Do a final proofreading of your poem double-checking your grammar, spelling, organization, and the clarity of your ideas.

NONFICTION ASSIGNMENT SHEET - *Great Gilly Hopkins*
(To be completed after reading the required nonfiction article)

Name _____ Date _____

Title of Nonfiction Read _____

Written By _____ Publication Date _____

I. Factual Summary: Write a short summary of the piece you read.

II. Vocabulary
   1. Which vocabulary words did you find difficult to understand?

   2. How did you resolve your lack of understanding of these words?

III. Interpretation: What was the main point the author wanted you to get from reading his work?

IV. Criticism
 1. Which points of the piece did you agree with or find easy to accept? Why?

 2. Which points of the piece did you disagree with or find difficult to believe? Why?

V. Personal Response: What do you think about this piece? OR How does this piece influence your ideas.

LESSON SIX

Objectives
1. To preview the vocabulary from Set 4
2. To give students practice reading orally
3. To evaluate students' oral reading
4. To prove previous predictions

Activity #1
Give students about ten minutes to do the prereading vocabulary work and preview study questions from Set 4.

Activity #2
Have students read One-Way Ticket and POW out loud in class. This will serve as a time for you to complete the following oral reading evaluation form for each student reading. You probably know the best way to select readers within your class; pick students at random, ask for volunteers, have students select each other, spin a spinner, etc. Reading of these chapters orally will better prepare your class for Writing Assignment #2 which follows in Lesson 7.

Activity #3
Have students retrieve their earlier predictions. Were they accurate? Perhaps you may want to reward those students who were accurate with some small prize.

ORAL READING EVALUATION - *The Great Gilly Hopkins*

Name _____ Class____ Date _____

SKILL	EXCELLENT	GOOD	AVERAGE	FAIR	POOR
Fluency	5	4	3	2	1
Clarity	5	4	3	2	1
Audibility	5	4	3	2	1
Pronunciation	5	4	3	2	1
_____	5	4	3	2	1
_____	5	4	3	2	1

Total _____ Grade _____

Comments:

LESSON SEVEN

Objectives
1. To review the main events and ideas and vocabulary from Set 4
2. To preview study questions and prereading vocabulary work for Set 5
3. To give students the opportunity to express personal ideas in writing

Activity #1
Have students glance over the vocabulary from Set 4. Write each of the ten words separately on the chalkboard leaving space beneath each one, or on separate pieces of newsprint taped to the wall around the room. Divide the class into ten teams or pairs. Have each team list as many synonyms for their assigned word as they can, beneath it, on the chalkboard or newsprint. Give them a time limit and reward the team with the most correct synonyms. It is up to you to decide if you want them to be able to refer to a thesaurus or dictionary first. If possible, you could have the students give an at least one antonym for their word, also.

Activity #2
Review the main ideas and events from Set 4 by asking your class to decide which of the earlier techniques they would like to use for review, or devise a new one.

Activity #3
In small groups, have students preview prereading vocabulary and study guide questions for Set 5. Assign reading of these chapters to be completed by class meeting for Lesson Nine.

Activity #4
Distribute Writing Assignment #2 and discuss directions in detail. Give students the remainder of the class time to work on this assignment.

WRITING ASSIGNMENT #2 - *The Great Gilly Hopkins*

PROMPT
Now that you have read the chapter called One-Way Ticket, you know that Gilly runs away to the local bus station to try to board a bus to San Francisco to find her mother. When William Earnest sees what she is doing, he pleads with her to stay. She feels she must leave her foster home at Maime Trotter's to go to live with her mother in California. Your assignment is to design a MISSING POSTER appealing for Gilly's immediate return to Thompson Park.

PREWRITING
Your poster should carry all the usual information that a MISSING POSTER would contain such as: clarity, appeal, picture of the missing person, last place seen and direction headed, physical description, including any remarkable features, clothing last seen wearing, phone number of agency or persons that can be reached if she is found, and any other information that you feel would help identify Gilly and assist in her speedy return to Maime Trotter's. Your poster must fit on an 8 1/2" by 11" sheet of paper or index paper.

DRAFTING
You need to make a few basic decisions concerning your poster. What size will the graphic representation of the likeness of Gilly be? Will you have a background? What will be the attention-getter in your poster? How can you make all your information appealing for Gilly's return fit on one page? How will you layout or design your poster? How will it look on the page? What type lettering will you use? Once you have decided these things, you can put pencil to paper and make a rough draft of your poster.

PROMPT
When you finish the rough draft of your poster, ask a student who sits near you to look over it. After reviewing your rough draft, he\she should tell you what he\she liked best about your work, and ways in which your work could be improved. Reread your paper considering your critic's comments, and make the corrections you think are necessary.

PROOFREADING
Do a final proofreading of your poster double-checking your design layout, spelling, organization, and the clarity of your ideas.

LESSON EIGHT

Objectives
1. To introduce alliteration, simile, metaphor, and personification as figures of speech
2. To have students locate figurative language in the text
3. To create original figures of speech and illustrate them

Activity #1
Tell the class you are going to read a few sentences to them from their novel. Ask them to listen carefully and try to identify similarities between the sentences or see if they can identify what they are examples of:

- To Gilly it seemed like a hundred years.
- She could curl up her whole body like a tiny sightless kitten.
- Gilly turned to face this mountain smelling of Johnson baby powder.
- If birth was a sleep and a forgetting, what was death?
- Why did her heart feel like a lump of poorly mashed potatoes?
- The ice in her frozen brain rumbled and cracked.
- The frog-eyed filcher, wild-eyed William, the goose-brained godfather

Point out that these are all comparisons or descriptions using figurative language from this book. List these four types of figurative language on the board, give further examples, and discuss each type.

Activity #2
Perhaps you could cite some examples from familiar songs. Ask why they think any author or lyricist would use them? Do they use them? Why? In what way does using them enhance speaking or writing or the understanding of each of these. As a whole group, have students give you examples they can think of and then have them locate a few in any part of the text they have read. Allow them to come to the board and write these. When you are satisfied with the students' ability to recognize and distinguish among them, go to the next activity.

Activity #3
Divide the class into small groups of three or four. Have each group assign a recorder. Give them a couple of sheets of paper. Ask each group to locate as many of these figures of speech as they can from the text. Giving them a time constraint is an option. It could be a race, you are the judge. You may want to rule out using the ones that are posted on the board. It's up to you. Wrap this activity up by having the group with the **most** read their list aloud. Decide as a whole group if indeed each one is correct. Have all groups check off the ones that are read that they also found. Allow every group to read any that have not yet been mentioned. You could give rewards for first, second, third place, etc.

Activity #4

Have students create an example of each of these figures of speech. They could be individual sentences or you could require them to write a short paragraph using two or three. Base this on the ability level of your students or the time available. Create one together as a model. If there is time, have them illustrate it with original art work or magazine pictures. Save finished products for display. They could do this part as homework.

FIGURATIVE LANGUAGE TEST - *The Great Gilly Hopkins*

I. Read the following examples of figurative language. Label each one separately with either an **S** for simile, **P** for personification, an **M** for metaphor, or an **A** for alliteration. **Circle** the one that contains an example of more than one.

1. Gilly had a vision of herself sailing around the living room of the foster home on her right foot like an ice skater,_____
2. The door had opened, and a huge hippopotamus of a woman was filling the doorway._____
3. Not that she expected this bale of blubber to manage her real name._____
4. Listening to that woman was like licking ice cream off the carton._____
5. The fat woman was eating it up like a hot-fudge sundae with all the nuts._____
6. She yanked open the top left drawer, pulling out a broken comb, which she viciously jerked through the wilderness on her head._____
7. She felt heavier with each step, like a condemned prisoner walking an endless last mile._____
8. The basketball kissed the rim but refused to go in for her. _____
9. They were yelping like hurt puppies._____
10. Gilly beared down on the girl like a child-eating ogre._____
11. I'd turn from Gilly into gorgeous, gracious, good, glorious, Galadriel._____
12. It was almost as though she were meddling in another person's brain._____
13. Mr. Randolph's face looked like a child's before a wrapped-up present.____
14. The music of the words rolled up and burst across Gilly like waves upon a beach. _____
15. Gilly's voice was sharp like the jagged edge of a tin-can top._____
16. Agnes went as stiff as a dry sponge._____
17. He was rattling the tray so hard that the milk was threatening to jump the edge._____
18. He turned around to grin shyly at Gilly as though carrying the crown of England._____
19. W.E. leaned back and let fly -"pow"-for another swooping, soaring, slowly spiraling, skimming superflight._____
20. He marched up the stairs as though he were the President of the United States._____

II. List one example of your own for each type of figurative language. They can be original or from your favorite songs or poetry.

III. Illustrate your favorite example of figurative language from those listed.

ANSWER KEY- FIGURATIVE LANGUAGE TEST - *The Great Gilly Hopkins*

I.
1. S
2. M
3. M
4. S
5. S
6. M
7. S
8. P
9. S
10. S
11. A
12. S
13. S
14. P, S
15. S
16. S
17. P
18. S
19. A
20. S

II. Answers will vary.

III. Creative response.

LESSON NINE

Objectives
1. To review the main events and ideas from Set 5
2. To preview study questions and prereading vocabulary work for Set 6
3. To give students the opportunity to work on their MISSING POSTERS

Activity #1
Hand out four slips of paper or cards to each student that have the letters A,B,C, or D on them. A good idea is to use different color cards for each letter. Use the multiple choice study guide questions and answers on Set 5 for an oral review. Read the question (and/ or show it on the overhead). Then give students the four possible answers, labeling them A, B, C, or D (or show on overhead again). Students respond by holding up the card with what they think is the correct answer. This is one variety of Every Student Response. Remind students not to look at what others are holding up, but to simply display the card of their choice. This is a quick indicator of students' comprehension. You can make it somewhat different by requiring complete silence and having them read the questions silently from the overhead, or make it more mysterious (fun?) by blindfolding everyone and have them hold up a certain number of fingers per answer instead of using the cards. You can also review vocabulary in this way by providing students with four possible definition responses per word.

Activity #2
In small groups, have students preview prereading vocabulary and study guide questions for Set 6. Assign reading of these chapters to be completed by the next class meeting time.

Activity #3
After adequate time has been spent on the earlier two activities, allow students to work on or to complete their Missing Posters.

LESSON TEN

Objectives
1. To review the main events and ideas from Set 6
2. To discuss the theme of belonging
3. To identify character traits
4. To determine if a character is static or dynamic

Activity #1
Use the multiple choice format of the study guide questions for Set 6 as a quiz to check that students have done the required reading and to review the main ideas of Set 6. Exchange papers for checking and discuss answers.

Activity #2
In small groups have students discuss what it means to belong. Encourage participation by asking the following type questions: To what can people belong? What needs are met by belonging to something? Is it important to have a sense of belonging? Can there be negative effects, as well as positive effects to belonging dependent on what type group one belongs to? How do values determine group behavior? Allow full class participation and encourage note-taking.

Activity #3
Reproduce the following graphic organizers so that each student has one of each of them. Make an overhead of each for you to use to model how to fill each of the charts out. Using Trotter as an example, fill out the character traits chart asking the class for input based on the listed categories. Next, fill out the Static/ Dynamic chart also using Trotter as an example of a static (not changing) character. Lead students to deduct that she is a static character rather than a dynamic character through use of the form. Inform students that they will be working on these graphic organizers for homework.

LESSON ELEVEN

Activity
Distribute Writing Assignment #3 and discuss the directions in detail. Give students the remainder of class time to work on this assignment. Inform students that these assignments are due by the Lesson Thirteen meeting time because you will be holding individual writing conferences with each of them.

Character_____

Physical Traits of Character	Actions of Character	Speech of Character	Thoughts and Feelings of Character	What others say about Character

Static or Dynamic

_____ is a **static/dynamic** character because

Character's Name (circle one)

Beginning Personality	Plot events that may /may not cause change					Ending Personality

WRITING ASSIGNMENT #3 - *The Great Gilly Hopkins*

PROMPT
Now that you have finished reading this book, you know that Gilly goes to live with her grandmother. She is fearful and uncertain about this arrangement, and begs Trotter to let her stay there with her and William Earnest. Even though Trotter has come to love Gilly very much. she feels that this move is in Gilly's best interest. Your assignment is to pretend to be Maime Trotter who writes a letter to Gilly defending her position.

PREWRITING
To begin with, create a list of reasons that support your objective of convincing Gilly that the move to her grandmother's is the best move for her overall. Come up with any and all possible arguments you can think of that will promote your choice in this matter. Review that last two chapters in the book for some ideas. Decide which are your strongest justifiable arguments, and which are less substantial. Organize your points from weaker to strongest utilizing your facts, opinions, and examples as evidence in support of your argument.

DRAFTING
Begin with an introductory paragraph in which you express your desire for Gilly to stay with her grandmother even though you love and care for her. Follow that with one paragraph for each of the main points you have to support your argument to convince Gilly that living with her grandmother is her best choice. Fill in each paragraph with your facts, opinions, and examples that support your decision. Then, write an ending paragraph that summarizes and restates your opinion and reinforces how you feel about Gilly as your final statement.

PROMPT
When you finish the rough draft of your paper, ask a student who sits near you to read it. After reading your rough draft, he or she should tell you what was best about your work, which parts were difficult to understand, and ways in which your work could be improved. Reread your paper considering your critic's comments, and make the corrections you think are necessary.

PROOFREADING
Do a final proofreading of your paper double-checking your grammar, spelling, organization, and the clarity of your ideas.

LESSON TWELVE

Objectives:
1. To give students the opportunity to share their nonfiction reading assignment
2. To give students the opportunity to share their MISSING POSTERS and poems

Activity #1
Allow students to share information learned from doing Writing Assignment #1 and the included nonfiction report. Encourage use of visuals.

Activity #2
Ask students individually, or in pairs (if they are more comfortable) to stand and share their Missing Posters. Post in a designated area. If the climate of friendly competition is right, vote on a few or one winning poster. Have the class decide on the criteria and the reward.

LESSON THIRTEEN

Objectives:
1. To discuss the ideas and themes from *The Great Gilly Hopkins* in greater detail
2. To have students exercise their interpretive and critical thinking skills
3. To relate some of the ideas in *The Great Gilly Hopkins* to the students' lives
4. To evaluate students' writing
5. To have students revise their Writing Assignment #3 papers

Activity #1
Choose the questions from the Extra Discussion Questions/Writing Assignments which seem most appropriate for your students. A class discussion of these questions is most effective if students have been given the opportunity to formulate answers to the questions prior to the discussion. To this end, you may either have all the students formulate answers to all the questions, divide your class into groups and assign one or more questions to each group, or you could assign one question to each student in your class. The option you choose will make a difference in the amount of class time needed for this activity.

Activity #2
While students are working on the above activity individually or in small groups, call students individually to your desk (or some other private area) to discuss their papers from
Writing Assignment #3. Use the following Writing Evaluation Form to help structure your conference. Give students a date when their revisions are due.

WRITING EVALUATION FORM - *The Great Gilly Hopkins*

Name _____ Date _____

Writing Assignment #1 for *The Great Gilly Hopkins* unit   Grade _____
Circle One For Each Item:

Description (paragraph 1)	excellent	good	fair	poor
Plans (body paragraphs)	excellent	workable	fair	not realistic
Conclusion	excellent	good	fair	poor
Grammar:	excellent	good	fair	poor (errors noted)
Spelling:	excellent	good	fair	poor (errors noted)
Punctuation:	excellent	good	fair	poor (errors noted)
Legibility:	excellent	good	fair	poor

Strengths:

Weaknesses:

Comments/Suggestions

LESSON FOURTEEN

Objectives:
1. To complete discussions begun in Lesson Thirteen
2. To allow students time to complete extra activities of their choice

Activity

After students have had ample time to formulate answers to the questions which they started in Lesson Thirteen, begin your class discussion of the questions and the ideas presented by the questions. Be sure students take notes during the discussion so they have information to study for the unit test.

EXTRA DISCUSSION QUESTIONS / WRITING ASSIGNMENTS - *The Great Gilly Hopkins*

<u>Interpretive</u>

1. From what point of view is this story told? How would the story change if told from only one character's point of view?

2. Identify the setting. How does it influence the plot of this novel?

3. Are the characters in *The Great Gilly Hopkins* stereotypes? If so, explain why an author would include stereotypes in a book. If they are not, explain how they merit individuality.

4. What are the main conflicts in the story, and how are they resolved?

5. What is foreshadowing? Give examples of foreshadowing used in *The Great Gilly Hopkins*.

6. Why do you think Agnes was introduced into the storyline? William Earnest?

7. Complete a character sketch for Gilly, Trotter, Miss Harris, and Courtney.

8. Formulate an accurate time line for Gilly's life beginning with when she was three years old and living with her mother.

9. Explain the role of each of these characters: Trotter, Miss Ellis, William Earnest, Mr. Randolph, Courtney, Nonnie, and Miss Harris.

10. Define climax. Next, summarize the main events leading up to **it** and the remaining events after **it** that create the resolution.

11. Locate examples of the dialect Trotter uses. Did its use influence your opinion of her?

12. How does Miss Harris' reaction to Gilly's poem affect Gilly?

<u>Critical</u>

13. Explain the significance of the title "*The Great Gilly Hopkins*."

14. What does Gilly mean when she says,"Are you going to stand by and let them rip me out and fold me up and fly me away? Leave me a string, Trotter, a thread, at least." ?

15. Compare the characters' lifestyle in northern Virginia and Maryland to your lifestyle.

Gilly Extra Discussion Questions Page 2

16. Why do you think Gilly decided to befriend Agnes and William Earnest after avoiding them initially?

17. Compare Agnes and Gilly. Why does Gilly bully her?

18. How and why does Gilly change during the course of this novel?

19. For what reason do you think Katherine Paterson includes some bad words in this book for young readers?

20. There are some religious issues and Biblical references in this novel. After reading a short biography of Katherine Paterson, tell why she is comfortable writing about these things.

21. Who is responsible for Gilly's happiness? Defend your answer.

22. Does Gilly have a right to be angry? to steal? to bully others? Explain your opinions.

23. Is the story of *The Great Gilly Hopkins* believable? Why or why not?

24. Discover what motivated Katherine Paterson to write a book about foster parenting.

25. Why does Katherine Paterson often tell us exactly what Gilly is thinking, as if it were Gilly speaking?

26. What universal themes appear in *The Great Gilly Hopkins*?

27. Do you agree or disagree with Trotter's statement to Gilly, "All that stuff about happy endings is lies. The only ending in this world is death." ?

28. Why do you think Gilly's mom abandoned her? How would you react if your mom deserted you and you had no idea about your father? How would you have coped? Explain.

29. Will Gilly "make Trotter proud" ? Support your answer.

30. Have you read any other books written by Katherine Paterson? How do they compare to *The Great Gilly Hopkins*? Which one is your favorite? Why?

Gilly Extra Discussion Questions Page 3

31. Were you surprised with Miss Harris' reaction to Gilly's poem and card? How did Gilly expect her to respond? What did you expect to happen in that type of situation? What does this tell us about Miss Harris' character?

32. Does Gilly hurt or help William Earnest?

33. Why does Gilly cling to her portrait of Courtney? Why doesn't she keep it out once she gets to Nonnie's?

Personal Response

34. Gilly experiences a number of different feelings dealing with her mother's desertion. Do you think this is abnormal? Have you ever been through a similar experience? Please share.

35. Have you ever had some sort of challenge presented to you like Gilly did- to learn to read well? How did it motivate you?

36. When the letter Gilly wrote to Courtney is acted upon by Miss Ellis, she is sorry she wrote it. Have you ever regretted doing something?

37. If you were William Earnest, how would you handle Gilly's initial intimidation?

38. If you were Agnes, how would you feel about Gilly? Have you ever had a friend like her? Share your experience.

39. Gilly becomes very upset with herself when she thinks she is turning soft. Are you hard on yourself about some weakness you think you have?

40. Did you ever help a younger sibling like Gilly helped William Earnest? What did you teach them or help them with? How did it make you feel?

41. Have you ever been the new kid in a school like Gilly? How did you handle it?

42. Gilly knows that stealing from Trotter and Mr. Randolph is wrong, but she still does it. Have you or someone you know ever gotten into a similar situation?

43. Do you decorate for the holidays with a big tree like Nonnie and Gilly prepared? What else do you do?

Gilly Extra Discussion Questions Page 4

Quotations

1. "I need to feel that you are willing to make some effort. This will be your third home in less than three years. I can't imagine that you enjoy all this moving around."

2. "Hey, there, I thought I heard y'all pull up. Welcome to Thompson Park, Gilly, honey."

3. "My Melvin, God rest him used to say that I never met a stranger. And if he'd said kid, he woulda been right. I never met a kid I couldn't make friends with."

4. "I like moving. It's boring to stay in one place."

5. The word "mother" triggered something deep in her stomach. She knew the danger signal. This was not the time to start dissolving like hot Jell-o.

6. "One thing we better get straight right now tonight. I won't have you making fun of that boy. One more thing. In this house we don't take the Lord's name in vain."

7. "I never touched one of those people in my life."

8. "Galadriel Hopkins, What a beautiful name! From Tolkein, of course."

9. "It was bad enough having to come to this broken-down old school but to be behind-to seem dumber than the rest of the kids-to have to appear a fool in front of...."

10. "We're not going to have fighting on the playground or anywhere else around here. You're at a new school now. You have a chance to-uh-make a new start. If you want to. If there's anyway I can help you- if you just feel like talking to somebody...."

11. "The agency wrote to me that you had moved. I wish it were to here. I miss you."

12. "Call me if you want anything. It ain't a shameful thing to need help, you know."

13. One man's trash is another man's treasure."

14. "No, no, Miss Gilly. Nobody's trying to make a fool of you. The real old English is at the front. Try over a way. Well, what do you think of Mr. Wordsworth, Miss Gilly?"

Gilly Extra Discussion Questions Page 5

15. "Dandelions."

16. "That is probably exactly the flower that Mr. Wordsworth meant, sure is the lowliest flower of them all."

17. "I'm coming, Courtney, trailing clouds of glory as I come."

18. "Baby-Face Teague, the frog-eyed filcher. Wild-eyed William, the goose-brained godfather. The possibilities were unlimited and delectable. The midget of the Mafia. The Orange Reader Squeezer. No. The Orange Squirt. "

19. "Pow. I say, it sure fly good."

20. "The look on Trotter's face was the one she had, in some deep part of her, longed to see all of her life, but not from someone like Trotter. That was not part of the plan."

21. "It was rather comfortable to go to school with no one yelling or cajoling- to know that your work was judged on its merits and was not affected by the teacher's personal opinion of the person doing the work. It was a little like throwing a basketball. If you aimed right you got it through the hoop; it was absolutely just and absolutely impersonal."

22. "No one had the right to cut herself off from other people like that. Just once, before she left this dump, she'd like to pull a wire inside that machine. Just once she'd like to see Harris-6 scream in anger-fall apart- break down."

23. "They're saying Black is beautiful! But the best that I can figger is that everyone who's saying so looks mighty like a   "

24. " You may find this hard to believe, Gilly, but you and I are very much alike. I don't mean in intelligence, although that is true, too. Both of us are smart, and we know it. But the thing that brings us closer than intelligence is anger. You and I are two of the angriest people I know. We do different things with our anger, of course. I was always taught to deny mine, which I did and still do. And that makes me envy you. Your anger is still up here on the surface where you can look it in the face, and make friends with it if you want."

25. "Between the craziness in the brown house and the craziness at school, she would become like W.E., soft and no good, and if there was anything her short life had taught her, it was that a person must be tough. Otherwise, you were had."

Gilly Extra Discussion Questoions Page 6

26. "People were so dumb sometimes you almost felt bad to take advantage of them- but not too bad. Not when it was your only way to get where you had to go."

27. "Trotter, baby, if you had half my brains you'd know to let the boy do things for himself. If I were going to stay here, I'd teach him how. You want to so hard, and you don't know how. Even the birds know to shove the babies out of the nest. If I were going to be here, I'd make a man of your little marshmallow. But I can't stay. I might go soft and stupid, too."

28. "Oh, mercy, mercy. The boy is always looking for some excuse to say I can't take care of myself so he can drag me over to his big house in Virginia."

29. "Come home, Gilly. Please come home! Please, please!"

30. "Somebody's got to favor Gilly for a little while, She's long overdue."

31. "You can't do that, Mrs. Trotter. You can't let them tear you to pieces. You're a foster mother and you can't afford to forget that."

32. "Are you going to stand by and let them rip me out and fold me up and fly me away?

33. "I'm not going to teach him to pick on people, just how to take care of himself. He can't come hiding behind your skirt every time someone looks at him cross-eyed."

34. "I promise not to die in your house. You have my solemn oath."

35. "As a matter of fact, this letter- this letter is the first direct word we've- I've had from my daughter in thirteen years. I didn't even know she had a ba-"

36. "She and your mother want you to go with your grandmother. Permanently."

37. "You bet I wouldn't. I don't understand why a smart girl like you goes around booby-trapping herself. You could have stayed here indefinitely, you know. They're both crazy about you."

38. "She wanted something Trotter had no power over. To stop being a 'foster child.' To be real without any quotation marks. To belong and to possess."

39. "No, Gilly, baby. It don't work that way. Like I tried to tell you at supper. Once the tugboat takes you out to the ocean liner, you got to get all the way on board. Can't straddle both decks."

Gilly Extra Discussion Questions Page 7

40. "You make me proud, hear?"

41. "That's not how you get to know people. Don't you know? You can't talk it out, you got to live into their lives, bad and good. You'll know me soon enough. What I want you to know."

42. "I told you on the phone that I'd come for Christmas and see for myself how the kid was doing... Look, I came, didn't I? Don't start pushing me before I'm hardly off the plane. My god, I've been gone thirteen years , and you still think you can tell me what to do."

43. "My sweet baby, ain't no one ever told you yet? I reckon I thought you had it all figured out. All that stuff about happy endings is lies. The only ending in this world is death. Now that might or might not be happy, but either way, you ain't ready to die, are you?"

44. "Sorry to make you wait. I'm ready to go home now."

LESSON FIFTEEN

Objectives:
1. To make available a knowledgeable professional resource on foster care
2. To compose thank you notes

Activity #1
In preparation for this lesson, have students prepare a list of questions about foster care.
Ask them to review the book for ideas or points of interest or curiosity. This could be part of your extra discussion/activities classes.

Activity #2
Contact a local social service agency that is willing to provide a speaker. (ideally, at the beginning of unit) Set the date up with the agency based on your timetable. If at all possible, allow the guest to preview *The Great Gilly Hopkins* or summarize for him/her prior to his visit. In this way, the speaker will know from what frame of reference the class, as an audience, is coming,

Activity #3
Have speaker address class on the many aspects of foster care. Perhaps past anonymous caseload examples could be shared. Encourage class members to share their questions and insights with the speaker.

Activity #4
After the speaker has finished, briefly review components of writing a *thank you* note. Assign these for homework. Perhaps you could generate a creative piece of stationery for students depicting the subject matter using Print Shop or Publisher software. Mail to speaker

LESSON SIXTEEN

<u>Objectives:</u>
To review all of the vocabulary work done in this unit

<u>Activity</u>

Choose one (or more) of the vocabulary review activities and spend your class period as directed in the activity. Some of the materials for these review activities are located in the Vocabulary Resource Section in this unit.

VOCABULARY REVIEW ACTIVITIES

1. Divide your class into two teams and have an old-fashioned spelling or definition bee.
2. Give each of your students (or students in groups of two, three or four) a *The Great Gilly Hopkins* Vocabulary Word Search Puzzle. The person (group) to find all of the vocabulary words in the puzzle first wins.
3. Give students a *The Great Gilly Hopkins* Vocabulary Word Search Puzzle without the word list. The person or group to find the most vocabulary words in the puzzle wins.
4. Use a *The Great Gilly Hopkins* Vocabulary Crossword Puzzle. Put the puzzle onto a transparency on the overhead projector (so everyone can see it), and do the puzzle together as a class.
5. Give students a *The Great Gilly Hopkins* Vocabulary Matching Worksheet to do.
6. Divide your class into two teams. Use *The Great Gilly Hopkins* vocabulary words with their letters jumbled as a word list. Student 1 from Team A faces off against Student 1 from Team B. You write the first jumbled word on the board. The first student (1A or 1B) to unscramble the word wins the chance for his or her team to score points. If 1A wins the jumble, go to student 2A and give him or her a definition. The student must give you the correct spelling of the vocabulary word which fits that definition. If he or she does, Team A scores a point, and you give student 3A a definition for which you expect a correctly spelled matching vocabulary word. Continue giving Team A definitions until some team member makes an incorrect response. An incorrect response sends the game back to the jumbled-word face off, this time with students 2A and 2B. Instead of repeating giving definitions, to the first few students of each team, continue with the student after the one who gave the last incorrect response on the team. For example, if Team B wins the jumbled-word face-off, and student 5B gave the last incorrect answer for Team B, you would start this round of definition questions with student 6B, and so on. The team with the most points wins!
7. Have students write a story in which they correctly use as many vocabulary words as possible. Have students read their compositions orally. Post the most original compositions on your bulletin board.

LESSON SEVENTEEN

Objective:
To review the main ideas presented in *The Great Gilly Hopkins*

Activity #1
Choose one of the review games/activities included in this unit and spend your class period as outlined there. Some materials for these activities are located in the Unit Resource section of this unit.

Activity #2
Remind students that the Unit Test will be in the next class meeting. Stress the review of the Study Guides and their class notes as a last minute, brush-up review for the unit test.

REVIEW GAMES/ACTIVITIES - *The Great Gilly Hopkins*

1. Ask the class to make up a unit test for *The Great Gilly Hopkins*. The test should have 4 sections: matching, true/false, short answer, and essay. Students may use 1/2 period to make the test and then swap papers and use the other 1/2 class period to take a test a classmate has devised. (open book) You may want to use the unit test included in this unit or take questions from the students' unit tests to formulate your own test.

2. Take 1/2 period for students to make up true and false questions (including the answers). Collect the papers and divide the class into two teams. Draw a big tic-tac-toe board on the chalk board. Make one team X and one team O. Ask questions to each side, giving each student one turn. If the question is answered correctly, that students' team's letter (X or O) is placed in the box. If the answer is incorrect, no mark is placed in the box. The object is to get three marks in a row like tic-tac-toe. You may want to keep track of the number of games won for each team.

3. Take 1/2 period for students to make up questions (true/false and short answer). Collect the questions. Divide the class into two teams. You'll alternate asking questions to individual members of teams A & B (like in a spelling bee). The question keeps going from A to B until it is correctly answered, then a new question is asked. A correct answer does not allow the team to get another question. Correct answers are +2 points; incorrect answers are -1 point.

4. Have students pair up and quiz each other from their study guides and class notes.

5. Give students a *The Great Gilly Hopkins* crossword puzzle to complete.

6. Divide your class into two teams. Use *The Great Gilly Hopkins* crossword words with their letters jumbled as a word list. Student 1 from Team A faces off against Student 1 from Team B. You write the first jumbled word on the board. The first student (1A or 1B) to unscramble the word wins the chance for his or her team to score points. If 1A wins the jumble, go to student 2A and give him or her a clue. The student must give you the correct word which matches that clue. If he or she does, Team A scores a point, and you give student 3A a clue for which you expect another correct response. Continue giving Team A clues until some team member makes an incorrect response. An incorrect response sends the game back to the jumbled-word face off, this time with students 2A and 2B. Instead of repeating giving clues to the first few students of each team, continue with the student after the one who gave the last incorrect response on the team. For example, if Team B wins the jumbled-word face-off, and student 5B gave the last incorrect answer for Team B, you would start this round of clue questions with student 6B, and so on.

UNIT TESTS

SHORT ANSWER UNIT TEST #1 - *The Great Gilly Hopkins*

I. Matching/Identify

____ 1. THREE   A.   Age when Gilly had last seen her mother

____ 2. NATIONAL APTITUDE   B.   Stolen from Trotter to mail letter to Courtney

____ 3. STAMP   C.   Nonnie's new hair coloring job

____ 4. SAN FRANCISCO   D.   Lives with her grandmother

____ 5. NONNIE   E.   W.E.'s favorite program

____ 6. GALADRIEL HOPKINS   F.   Gilly's destination

____ 7. MISS HARRIS   G.   Eleven year-old foster girl

____ 8. TUTUS   H.   Gilly was afraid to touch someone this color

____ 9. BLACK   I.   Ballerinas on Melvin's tie wore these

____ 10. KATHERINE PATERSON   J.   Poem is written for her

____ 11. RINSE   K.   Author

____ 12. CALIFORNIA   L.   Postmark on Courtney's postcard

____ 13. ANGER   M.   Emotion that Miss Harris and Gilly share

____ 14. AGNES STOKES   N.   Courtney's mother

____ 15. SESAME STREET   O.   Test Gilly scored highest on

The Great Gilly Hopkins Short Answer Unit Test 1 Page 2

II. Short Answer

1. Describe Galadriel Hopkins.

2. What is Gilly's first impression of Trotter?

3. Why is Gilly angry the morning Trotter is to take her to school?

4. What does she find as she is trying to straighten up Mr. Randolph's books?

5. When W.E. brings Gilly a tray of Trotter's cookies and milk, what plan does she devise?

6. How does Gilly try to 'get to' Miss Harris? Does Gilly get the expected response from her teacher? Explain.

7. Why and to whom does Gilly write at the end of the chapter, "Dust and Desperation"?

The Great Gilly Hopkins Short Answer Unit Test 1 Page 3

8. Where do the police take Gilly and what happens there?

9. How does Trotter handle the issue of the stolen money?

10. What does Gilly teach William Earnest?

11. What does the little lady claiming to be Gilly's grandmother tell her?

12. What is Mr. Randolph's farewell gift for Gilly?

13. What does Trotter share with Gilly that night when she comforts Gilly from her bad dream?

14. What does Miss Harris send to Gilly and why?

15. Why is Gilly shocked upon meeting Courtney? Why is Nonnie upset?

III. Essay

    Gilly changes during the course of this novel. Cite which events you think had the biggest impact on her and why.

The Great Gilly Hopkins Short Answer Unit Test 1 Page 5

IV. Vocabulary

Listen to the vocabulary words and spell them. After you have spelled all the words, go back and write down the definitions.

1.

2.

3.

4.

5.

6.

7.

8.

9.

10.

KEY: SHORT ANSWER UNIT TEST #1 - *The Great Gilly Hopkins*

I. Matching/Identify

A 1. THREE	A.	Age when Gilly had last seen her mother
O 2. NATIONAL APTITUDE	B.	Stolen from Trotter to mail letter to Courtney
B 3. STAMP	C.	Nonnie's new hair coloring job
F 4. SAN FRANCISCO	D.	Lives with her grandmother
N 5. NONNIE	E.	W.E.'s favorite program
G 6. GALADRIEL HOPKINS	F.	Gilly's destination
J 7. MISS HARRIS	G.	Eleven year-old foster girl
I 8. TUTUS	H.	Gilly was afraid to touch someone this color
H 9. BLACK	I.	Ballerinas on Melvin's tie wore these
K 10. KATHERINE PATERSON	J.	Poem is written for her
C 11. RINSE	K.	Author
L 12. CALIFORNIA	L.	Postmark on Courtney's postcard
M 13. ANGER	M.	Emotion that Miss Harris and Gilly share
D 14. AGNES STOKES	N.	Courtney's mother
E 15. SESAME STREET	O.	Test Gilly scored highest on

II. Short Answer

1. Describe Galadriel Hopkins.
   She is an eleven-year-old foster child who has been constantly moved around. This is her third placement in three years. She prides herself on being brilliant, clever, and hard to manage. Her nickname is Gruesome Gilly.

2. What is Gilly's first impression of Trotter?
   She thinks she is a hippopotamus of a woman with terrible teeth. She irritates Gilly with her warmth and familiar ways. She calls her a freak.

3. Why is Gilly angry the morning Trotter is to take her to school?
   She is upset because Trotter doesn't seem to notice how messy her hair looks and when she goes upstairs to fix it, Trotter asks her to make the beds.

4. What does she find as she is trying to straighten up Mr. Randolph's books?
   Two five dollar bills flutter down from the behind an encyclopedia.

5. When W.E. brings Gilly a tray of Trotter's cookies and milk, what plan does she devise?
   She suddenly decides that W.E. may come in handy someday and she entertains herself with possible criminal names for him. Immediately after she finishes her snack, she goes down and watches TV with him.

6. How does Gilly try to 'get to' Miss Harris? Does Gilly get the expected response from her teacher? Explain.
   She is disturbed by Miss Harris' seeming lack of emotional dependence on her class. She is too impersonal for Gilly and she wants to stir things up. She creates an illustrated poem that is very demeaning in a racial way towards Miss Harris' race. She anonymously places it in Miss Harris' math book early in the morning.

7. Why and to whom does Gilly write at the end of the chapter, "Dust and Desperation"?
   She writes a letter to her mother asking her to send her the needed money for a bus ticket so she can join her in California. She claims that Trotter is a religious fanatic, William Earnest is retarded, and that she is being mistreated.

8. Where do the police take Gilly and what happens there?
   The police come and take her to the police station. The police search her suitcase and find Trotter's address on the postcard from Courtney. They call Trotter. She and William Earnest show up to take her home.

9. How does Trotter handle the issue of the stolen money?
   She has Gilly return Mr. Randolph's money to him and then she makes Gilly earn back the remainder of the missing money through various jobs. The highest paying job is helping William Earnest with his homework.

10. What does Gilly teach William Earnest?
    She determines that W.E. needs to be able to defend himself and not hide behind Trotter anymore. She teaches him how to stick up for himself. He practices his newly learned strategy on Trotter.

11. What does the little lady claiming to be Gilly's grandmother tell her?
    She tells Gilly that she never knew she had a granddaughter.

12. What is Mr. Randolph's farewell gift for Gilly?
    He gives her the leather-bound book of poetry from which she read the Wordsworth poem.

13. What does Trotter share with Gilly that night when she comforts Gilly from her bad dream?
    She tells Gilly that Gilly's leaving is killing her, even though she isn't supposed to let her know how she feels. She tells Gilly to make her proud.

14. What does Miss Harris send to Gilly and why?
    She sends Gilly books written by J.R. Tolkein. She had meant to lend them to her when she was still at Thompson Park, but since Gilly had to leave she sends them as a remembrance of their time together.

15. Why is Gilly shocked upon meeting Courtney? Why is Nonnie upset?
    She doesn't look at all like the picture Gilly has treasured for so long. She only has enough clothes for a two day visit. It is revealed that Nonnie has sent her the money to return.

III. Composition answers will vary.

IV. Vocabulary

Choose ten of the vocabulary words to read orally for the vocabulary section of this unit test.

SHORT ANSWER UNIT TEST #2 *The Great Gilly Hopkins*

I. Matching/Identify

1. KATHERINE PATERSON	A.	Author of books Miss Harris sends Gilly
2. TEN	B.	Nickname main character gives herself
3. WORDSWORTH	C.	What Gilly called her card to Miss Harris
4. THOMPSON PARK	D.	Number of years since Nonnie heard from her daughter
5. HARRIS-6	E.	Gilly's new classroom
6. THIRTEEN	F.	Virus all except Gilly got on Thanksgiving
7. MASTERPIECE	G.	Foster home location in Maryland
8. THIRTY-FOUR	H.	Describes Courtney
9. FLU	I.	Emotion that Miss Harris and Gilly share
10. FLOWER CHILD	J.	Amount of money W.E. found for Gilly
11. ANGER	K.	Author
12. DANDELION	L.	Price of one-way ticket to San Francisco
13. ONE THIRTY- SIX SIXTY	M.	Money that fell from behind encyclopedia
14. GRUESOME GILLY	N.	Poet who wrote about the trailing clouds of glory
15. TOLKEIN	O.	Meanest flower that blows

The Great Gilly Hopkins Short Answer Unit Test 2 Page 2

II. Short Answer

1. Describe Galadriel Hopkins.

2. How does Maime Trotter greet her new foster child?

3. How does Trotter set Gilly straight about W.E. and her swearing?

4. Why is Gilly angry the morning Trotter is to take her to school?

5. Explain what happens on the playground at recess on Gilly's first day at her new school..

6. What does Gilly find as she is trying to straighten up Mr. Randolph's books?

7. When W.E. brings Gilly a tray of Trotter's cookies and milk, what plan does she devise?

8. Why does Gilly find it urgent to try to leave Thompson Park as soon as possible?

The Great Gilly Hopkins Short Answer Unit Test 2 Page 3

9. How does Gilly employ W.E. and Agnes in her first plan?

10. Why does Trotter send Gilly upstairs after Sunday dinner? What does she do?

11. What did Miss Ellis and Trotter argue about after Gilly's return from the police station?

12. Why was Gilly absent the Tuesday and Wednesday before Thanksgiving?

13. Who shows up at Trotter's on Thanksgiving? Describe the scene at Trotter's that day.

14. Who is waiting at Trotter's when she and W.E. return from school? What news does she bring? Describe the dinner scene that night at Trotter's.

15. Why is Gilly shocked upon meeting Courtney? Why is Nonnie upset? How does Gilly deal with her fear and disappointment?

The Great Gilly Hopkins Short Answer Unit Test 2 Page 4

III. Essay

    Who is responsible for Gilly's happiness? Defend your answer.

The Great Gilly Hopkins Short Answer Unit Test 2 Page 5

IV. Vocabulary

Listen to the vocabulary words and spell them. After you have spelled all the words, go back and write down the definitions.

1.

2.

3.

4.

5.

6.

7.

8.

9.

10.

KEY: SHORT ANSWER UNIT TEST 2 *The Great Gilly Hopkins*

I. Matching

K 1. KATHERINE PATERSON   A.   Author of books Miss Harris sends Gilly

M 2. TEN   B.   Nickname main character gives herself

N 3. WORDSWORTH   C.   What Gilly called her card to Miss Harris

G 4. THOMPSON PARK   D.   Number of years since Nonnie heard from Courtney

E 5. HARRIS-6   E.   Gilly's new classroom

D 6. THIRTEEN   F.   Virus all except Gilly got on Thanksgiving

C 7. MASTERPIECE   G.   Foster home location in Maryland

J 8. THIRTY-FOUR   H.   Describes Courtney

F 9. FLU   I.   Emotion that Miss Harris and Gilly share

H 10. FLOWER CHILD   J.   Amount of money W.E. found for Gilly

I 11. ANGER   K.   Author

O 12. DANDELION   L.   Price of one-way ticket to San Francisco

L 13. ONE THIRTY SIX SIXTY   M.   Money that fell from behind encyclopedia

B 14. GRUESOME GILLY   N.   Poet who wrote about the trailing clouds of glory

A 15. TOLKEIN   O.   Meanest flower that blows

II. Short Answer

1. Describe Galadriel Hopkins.
   She is an eleven-year-old foster child who has been constantly moved around. This is her third placement in three years. She prides herself on being brilliant, clever, and hard to manage. Her nickname is Gruesome Gilly.

2. How does Maime Trotter greet her new foster child?
   Maime claims to never have met a kid she couldn't make friends with. She tells Gilly she belongs there now and calls her Gilly, honey.

3. How does Trotter set Gilly straight about W.E. and her swearing?
   She lets Gilly know she will not tolerate taking the Lord's name in vain in her house and that in no way is she to hurt W.E. He is under her protection now, and ain't nobody on earth gonna hurt him.

4. Why is Gilly angry the morning Trotter is to take her to school?
   She is upset because Trotter doesn't seem to notice how messy her hair looks and when she goes upstairs to fix it, Trotter asks her to make the beds.

5. Explain what happens on the playground at recess on Gilly's first day at her new school..
   She snags a loose basketball and she runs with it and shoots to her heart's delight. The boys chase her and tackle her to the ground. There are six of them to one of her. They are all marched to the principal's office by Miss Harris where they are lectured. Mr. Evans detains Gilly and offers her help and reminds her she can make a new start there. He also insists on no fighting at this school anywhere.

6. What does Gilly find as she is trying to straighten up Mr. Randolph's books?
   Two five dollar bills flutter down from the behind an encyclopedia.

7. When W.E. brings Gilly a tray of Trotter's cookies and milk, what plan does she devise?
   She suddenly decides that W.E. may come in handy someday and she entertains herself with possible criminal names for him. Immediately after she finishes her snack, she goes down and watches TV with him.

8. Why does Gilly find it urgent to try to leave Thompson Park as soon as possible?
   She is afraid that she is turning soft. This place is messing her up and she needs to stay tough.

9. How does Gilly employ W.E. and Agnes in her first plan?
   Agnes acts as a guard outside Mr. Randolph's house, while Gilly hoists W.E. up so he can look behind the books in the bookcase near where the other money fell out. He discovers a wad of bills and hands them over to Gilly. She leads him to believe it is all a good surprise for Mr. Randolph.

10. Why does Trotter send Gilly upstairs after Sunday dinner? What does she do?
    Mr. Randolph's son will be coming soon and there is a stain on his tie. Trotter sends Gilly upstairs to get one of her deceased husband's ties for him. Gilly sees cash lying in Trotter's open purse and takes it. This is all she needs to be able to buy the bus ticket for California. She goes upstairs to pack after Trotter settles on the couch for an afternoon nap.

11. What did Miss Ellis and Trotter argue about?
    Miss Ellis wants to remove Gilly from Trotter's foster home and Trotter insists that she stay. They put the choice in Gilly's hands and she chooses to stay until her mother comes for her.

12. Why was Gilly absent the Tuesday and Wednesday before Thanksgiving?
    Everyone in the house, including Mr. Randolph, were sick with the flu. Gilly was taking care of all of them.

13. Who shows up at Trotter's on Thanksgiving? Describe the scene at Trotter's that day.
    A little old lady with a Southern accent claiming to be Gilly's grandmother appears at their door on Thanksgiving. William Earnest cries for Gilly after he wets his bed. Mr. Randolph is sleeping on a cot in the dining room. Trotter is a wreck and falls over, pinning Gilly beneath her. The place is a disaster area.

14. Who is waiting at Trotter's when she and W.E. return from school? What news does she bring? Describe the dinner scene that night at Trotter's.
    Miss Ellis brings the news that Gilly's mother wants her to go to live with her grandmother in Virginia. She has spoken with Courtney on the telephone. Trotter fixes a grand dinner of her special fried chicken. W.E. is crying openly and the rest of them are very quiet and sad thinking of Gilly's next day departure.

15. Why is Gilly shocked upon meeting Courtney? Why is Nonnie upset? How does Gilly deal with her fear and disappointment?
    She doesn't look at all like the picture Gilly has treasured for so long. She only has enough clothes for a two day visit. It is revealed that Nonnie has sent her the money to return. She excuses herself to the bathroom and tries to throw up. When that is unsuccessful, she dials Trotter's number and begs to come home. Trotter gives her the strength and encouragement to go out and meet with her mother and grandmother and go home with them.

III. Essay
   Answers will vary.

IV. Vocabulary
   Choose ten of the vocabulary words read orally for the vocabulary section of the test.

ADVANCED SHORT ANSWER UNIT TEST - *The Great Gilly Hopkins*

I. Matching

____ 1. THREE A. Age when Gilly had last seen her mother

____ 2. NATIONAL APTITUDE B. Stolen from Trotter to mail letter to Courtney

____ 3. STAMP C. Nonnie's new hair coloring job

____ 4. SAN FRANCISCO D. Lives with her grandmother

____ 5. NONNIE E. W.E.'s favorite program

____ 6. GALADRIEL HOPKINS F. Gilly's destination

____ 7. MISS HARRIS G. Eleven year-old foster girl

____ 8. TUTUS H. Gilly was afraid to touch someone this color

____ 9. BLACK I. Ballerinas on Melvin's tie wore these

____ 10. KATHERINE PATERSON J. Poem is written for her

____ 11. RINSE K. Author

____ 12. CALIFORNIA L. Postmark on Courtney's postcard

____ 13. ANGER M. Emotion that Miss Harris and Gilly share

____ 14. AGNES STOKES N. Courtney's mother

____ 15. SESAME STREET O. Test Gilly scored highest on

The Great Gilly Hopkins Advanced Short Answer Unit Test Page 2

II. Short Answer
1. How and why does Gilly change during the course of this novel?

2. Why do you think the author introduced William Earnest into the plot?

3. Do you agree or disagree with the following Trotter quote? " All that stuff about happy endings is lies. The only ending in this world is death." Explain.

4. How does Miss Harris' reaction to Gilly's poem affect Gilly?

5. Is Gilly and Nonnie's relationship similar or different from Gilly's relationship with Trotter? Support your answer.

6. Will Gilly "make Trotter proud"? Support your answer.

The Great Gilly Hopkins Advanced Short Answer Unit Test Page 3

III. Quotations: Explain the importance and meaning of the following quotations.

1. The word "mother" triggered something deep in her stomach. She knew the danger signal. This was not the time to start dissolving like hot Jell-o.

2. "I'm coming, Courtney, trailing clouds of glory as I come."

3. "The look on Trotter's face was the one she had, in some deep part of her, longed to see all of her life, but not from someone like Trotter. That was not part of the plan."

4. "It was rather comfortable to know that your work was judged on its merits and was not affected by the teacher's personal opinion of the person doing the work.

5. "Your anger is still up here on the surface where you can look it in the face, and make friends with it if you want."

6. "People were so dumb sometimes you almost felt bad to take advantage of them- but not too bad. Not when it was your only way to get where you had to go."

The Great Gilly Hopkins Advanced Short Answer Unit Test Page 4

7. "Somebody's got to favor Gilly for a little while, She's long overdue."

8. "No, Gilly, baby. It don't work that way. Like I tried to tell you at supper. Once the tugboat takes you out to the ocean liner, you got to get all the way on board. Can't straddle both decks."

The Great Gilly Hopkins Advanced Short Answer Unit Test Page 5

IV. Vocabulary

Listen to the vocabulary words and write them down. After you have written down all the words, write a paragraph in which you use all the words. The paragraph must in some way relate to *The Great Gilly Hopkins*.

MULTIPLE CHOICE UNIT TEST 1 - *The Great Gilly Hopkins*

I. Matching

1. THREE		A.	Age when Gilly had last seen her mother
2. NATIONAL APTITUDE		B.	Stolen from Trotter to mail letter to Courtney
3. STAMP		C.	Nonnie's new hair coloring job
4. SAN FRANCISCO		D.	Lives with her grandmother
5. NONNIE		E.	W.E.'s favorite program
6. GALADRIEL HOPKINS		F.	Gilly's destination
7. MISS HARRIS		G.	Eleven year-old foster girl
8. TUTUS		H.	Gilly was afraid to touch someone this color
9. BLACK		I.	Ballerinas on Melvin's tie wore these
10. KATHERINE PATERSON		J.	Poem is written for her
11. RINSE		K.	Author
12. CALIFORNIA		L.	Postmark on Courtney's postcard
13. ANGER		M.	Emotion that Miss Harris and Gilly share
14. AGNES STOKES		N.	Courtney's mother
15. SESAME STREET		O.	Test Gilly scored highest on

The Great Gilly Hopkins Multiple Choice Unit Test 1 page 2

II. Multiple Choice

1. Miss Ellis is
   a. Gilly's teacher from Hollywood Gardens.
   b. Gilly's case worker.
   c. Gilly's long lost aunt from California.
   d. Gilly's new foster mother.

2. Maime Trotter says she never met a kid she couldn't make friends with.
   a. false
   b. true

3. Gilly starts out with Maime Trotter by
   a. being sweet and polite when talked to by anyone.
   b. holding the door open for Miss Ellis and her.
   c. acting rude and banging on the piano.
   d. all of the above

4. What two things does Trotter set Gilly straight on right from the start?
   a. her swearing
   b. hurting William Earnest
   c. cleaning detail
   d. both a and b
   e. both a and c

5. Gilly is excited to have an intelligent teacher and be placed in the challenging sixth grade at Thompson Park.
   a. true
   b. false

6. Agnes Stokes is
   a. the only other white girl that is in Gilly's class.
   b. a popular girl from Gilly's class.
   c. a red-haired girl from the other sixth grade class.
   d. Gilly's friend from Hollywood Gardens.

The Great Gilly Hopkins Multiple Choice Unit Test 1 page 3

7. When Gilly starts reading the Wordsworth poem, Mr. Randolph
   a. can't remember which poem it is that he used to love so dearly.
   b. gets up and walks slowly around the room to the rhthym of the words.
   c. breaks down into tears.
   d. recites it along with her reading it in a soft and warm voice.

8. Gilly is comfortable with Trotter's praise and kindness.
   a. true
   b. false

9. Gilly decides she must stir Miss Harris up by
   a. putting a whoopie cushion on her seat before she sits down.
   b. refusing to turn in her homework.
   c. creating a card with racial slurs and anonymously leaving it for her.
   d. letting the air out of her tires.

10. After the incident with Miss Harris, Gilly decides
    a. she's got to get out of Thompson Park as soon as possible before she turns soft.
    b. to get back at Miss Harris again in some other way.
    c. she'll play a trick on Trotter too.
    d. to get back at the principal too.

11. How does Gilly use William Earnest and Agnes in her next plan?
    a. Agnes is to put the new card on Miss Harris' desk while she takes W.E. to his room.
    b. Agnes is to distract W.E. while Gilly does what she needs to do.
    c. William Earnest hides the money while Agnes looks for more.
    d. Agnes stands guard while W.E. looks for the money.

12. What does Gilly do when she is sent upstairs to Trotter's room?
    a. She gets a gaudy tie of Melvin's for Mr. Randolph.
    b. She steals money out of Maime's open purse.
    c. She makes the beds that are unmade.
    d. Both a and b

13. Why doesn't Gilly take the first ticket the bus station clerk issues?
    a. It doesn't leave for four hours and she wants to get going sooner.
    b. She wants to go to Washington D.C. first.
    c. She can't decide what to do next.
    d. She gets too nervous and makes a mistake.

The Great Gilly Hopkins Multiple Choice Unit Test 1 page 4

14. When Gilly comes home from school the day after she attempts to leave, she overhears
    a. Miss Ellis and Trotter arguing.
    b. William Earnest crying because he has to leave Trotter.
    c. a phone call from someone in Virginia.
    d. Trotter say that she just can't keep Gilly any longer after she has stolen from her.

15. What does Gilly teach William Earnest?
    a. Gilly teaches William Earnest how to play basketball.
    b. She helps him do origami.
    c. She tells him the ways to drive a teacher wild.
    d. Gilly teaches W.E. how to stand up for himself.

16. The visitor who shows up at Trotter's on Thanksgiving Day is
    a. Gilly's mother, Courtney.
    b. Gilly's grandmother, Courtney's mother.
    c. Miss Harris inquiring about Gilly's absences.
    d. none of the above

17. What news does Miss Ellis bring to Trotter's the Monday after Thanksgiving.
    a. Courtney has called her from California.
    b. Courtney wants Gilly to live with her grandmother in Virginia.
    c. Both a and b
    d. None of the above

18. What does Mr. Randolph give Gilly for a farewell gift?
    a. He gives her the money she repaid him.
    b. He promises he will come to see her when his son from Virginia gets him.
    c. He gives her the poetry book from which she read the Wordsworth poem.
    d. He gives her the encyclopedia that hid the two five dollar bills.

19. Gilly writes to William Earnest about
    a. the horses they own and how she takes care of them.
    b. how rich they are in Virginia.
    c. both a and b
    d. her new school and teachers.

The Great Gilly Hopkins Multiple Choice Unit Test 1 page 5

20. Why is Gilly stunned and upset at the airport?
    a. Courtney looks nothing like her picture.
    b. Nonnie sent Courtney the money to fly home to see her.
    c. Courtney only plans to stay for two days.
    d. All of the above

The Great Gilly Hopkins Multiple Choice Unit Test 1 page 6

III. Quotations: Identify the speaker:

A= Gilly   B= Trotter   C= William Earnest   D= Miss Ellis   E= Mr. Randolph

F= Nonnie   G= Courtney   H= Miss Harris

1. "One thing we better get straight right now tonight. I won't have you making fun of that boy. One more thing. In this house we don't take the Lord's name in vain."

2. "Call me if you want anything. It ain't a shameful thing to need help, you know."

3. "That is probably exactly the flower that Mr. Wordsworth meant, sure is the lowliest flower of them all."

4. "I'm coming, Courtney, trailing clouds of glory as I come."

5. "Pow. I say, it sure fly good."

6. "You may find this hard to believe, Gilly, but you and I are very much alike. I don't mean in intelligence, although that is true, too. Both of us are smart, and we know it. But the thing that brings us closer than intelligence is anger. You and I are two of the angriest people I know. We do different things with our anger, of course. I was always taught to deny mine, which I did and still do. And that makes me envy you. Your anger is still up here on the surface where you can look it in the face, and make friends with it if you want."

7. "Oh, mercy, mercy. The boy is always looking for some excuse to say I can't take care of myself so he can drag me over to his big house in Virginia."

8. "Come home, Gilly. Please come home! Please, please!"

9. "You can't do that , Mrs. Trotter. You can't let them tear you to pieces. You're a foster mother and you can't afford to forget that."

10. "As a matter of fact, this letter- this letter is the first direct word we've- I've had from my daughter in thirteen years. I didn't even know she had a ba-"

11. "You bet I wouldn't. I don't understand why a smart girl like you goes around booby-trapping herself. You could have stayed here indefinitely, you know. They're both crazy about you."

The Great Gilly Hopkins Multiple Choice Unit Test 1 page 7

12. "She wanted something Trotter had no power over. To stop being a "foster child". To be real without any quotation marks. To belong and to possess."

13. "You make me proud, hear?"

14. "I told you on the phone that I'd come for Christmas and see for myself how the kid was doing... Look, I came, didn't I? Don't start pushing me before I'm hardly off the plane. My god, I've been gone thirteen years, and you still think you can tell me what to do."

15. "My sweet baby, ain't no one ever told you yet? I reckon I thought you had it all figured out. All that stuff about happy endings is lies. The only ending in this world is death. Now that might or might not be happy, but either way, you ain't ready to die, are you?"

The Great Gilly Hopkins Multiple Choice Unit Test 1 page 8

IV. Vocabulary (Matching)

1. SEETHED	A.	hearable
2. PSYCHOLOGISTS	B.	pure
3. QUAVERING	C.	hug
4. PIOUSLY	D.	proved
5. VARIATIONS	E.	designed with letters
6. SELF-RIGHTEOUS	F.	useless
7. ANONYMOUS	G.	endless
8. CULINARY	H.	unsigned
9. AUDIBLE	I.	raged; fumed
10. FLUTED	J.	in a holy manner
11. ENTHRALLED	K.	concerning cooking
12. CONFIRMED	L.	therapists
13. FLIRTATION	M.	having grooves
14. FUTILE	N.	teasing
15. AGONY	O.	misery
16. MONOGRAMMED	P.	meekness; surrender
17. PERPETUAL	Q.	trembling
18. EMBRACE	R.	fascinated
19. SUBMISSION	S.	loaded down
20. LADEN	T.	variety

MULTIPLE CHOICE UNIT TEST 2 - *The Great Gilly Hopkins*

I. Matching

1. KATHERINE PATERSON
2. TEN
3. WORDSWORTH
4. THOMPSON PARK
5. HARRIS-6
6. THIRTEEN
7. MASTERPIECE
8. THIRTY-FOUR
9. FLU
10. FLOWER CHILD
11. ANGER
12. DANDELION
13. ONE THIRTY- SIX SIXTY
14. GRUESOME GILLY
15. TOLKEIN

A. Author of books Miss Harris sends Gilly
B. Nickname main character gives herself
C. What Gilly called her card to Miss Harris
D. Number of years since Nonnie heard from her daughter
E. Gilly's new classroom
F. Virus all except Gilly got on Thanksgiving
G. Foster home location in Maryland
H. Describes Courtney
I. Emotion that Miss Harris and Gilly share
J. Amount of money W.E. found for Gilly
K. Author
L. Price of one-way ticket to San Francisco
M. Money that fell from behind encyclopedia
N. Poet who wrote about the trailing clouds of glory
O. Meanest flower that blows

The Great Gilly Hopkins Multiple Choice Unit Test 2 page 2

II. Multiple Choice

1. Galadriel Hopkins is
   a. a foster child.
   b. an eleven-year old girl.
   c. brilliant, clever, and hard to manage.
   d. all of the above

2. Maime Trotter says she never met a kid she couldn't make friends with.
   a. true
   b. false

3. The man who comes to supper is
   a. Maime's neighbor, Mr. Randolph.
   b. Maime's son who lives across town.
   c. Gilly's case worker, Mr. Rudolph.
   d. the minister at Maime's Baptist church.

4. At the end of the second chapter, Gilly promises herself she will
   a. run away as soon as she has enough money.
   b. write to her aunt to come and get her.
   c. find her mother, Courtney Hopkins.
   d. start a new life here in Thompson Park

5. Gilly is angry the morning Trotter is to take her to school because
   a. she thinks Trotter is a religious fanatic.
   b. she doesn't think Trotter cares how she looks for her first day at school.
   c. Trotter asks her to make the beds while she is upstairs
   d. Both b and c

6. During recess on her first day at Thompson Park, Gilly
   a. asks the teacher on duty if she can help her.
   b. steals a basketball from some boys and gets in a fight.
   c. calls some black kids bad names.
   d. makes three new friends.

The Great Gilly Hopkins Multiple Choice Unit Test 2 page 3

7. Gilly is sent to Mr. Randolph's after supper to
   a. locate something to read other than Maime's Bible.
   b. try to find the stepladder to clean the chandelier.
   c. clean up his house for him.
   d. none of the above

8. When asked for her opinion of the Wordsworth poem she just read, Gilly says it is
   a. beautiful.
   b. stupid.
   c. too long.
   d. boring.

9. When W.E. brings Gilly a tray of milk and cookies, she
   a. thanks him nicely and shuts the door behind him.
   b. scares him by jumping out from under the bed.
   c. slams the door in his face.
   d. devises a plan to win him over for her own good.

10. How does Gilly manage to get back in Mr. Randolph's house again with him there?
    a. She sneaks in when he is sleeping.
    b. She comes to get him for supper and waits while he washes up before leaving.
    c. She offers to clean his house for him and since he is blind he can't see what she is up to.
    d. She comes over to borrow the stepladder to clean Trotter's chandelier.

11. When Gilly voices her opinion about the minister to Trotter
    a. Trotter says she is thinking of going to the black baptist church with Mr. Randolph.
    b. Trotter explodes and says," who am I to pass judgment on the Lord's anointed?"
    c. William Earnest agrees with Gilly so Trotter wants to find a better church for them.
    d. Trotter very patiently explains that he is new and hasn't learned the ways yet.

12. The last thing that happens at the police station is
    a. Miss Ellis shows up to take Gilly to Social Services.
    b. The police search through Gilly's suitcase.
    c. Trotter and William Earnest come in a taxi to take Gilly home.
    d. Mr. Randolph calls the police station wondering where his neighbors have gone.

The Great Gilly Hopkins Multiple Choice Unit Test 2 page 4

13. How does Trotter manage Gilly's debt?
    a. She has her ask Mr. Randolph for a loan.
    b. She lists the rates by which Gilly can earn back the missing money.
    c. She signs Gilly up at the church for community service.
    d. She has Gilly write an apology to Mr. Randolph and to her.

14. When Trotter finds out what Gilly is teaching William Earnest she
    a. is proud.
    b. is worried.
    c. can't watch.
    d. all of the above

15. Select the one thing that did not happen at Trotters on Thanksgiving Day.
    a. An uninvited visitor shows up at the door.
    b. Mr. Randolph's son came looking for him.
    c. William Earnest wet his pants and bed.
    d. Trotter fell on Gilly and squashed her.

16. What does Trotter share with Gilly that night when she comforts Gilly from her bad dream?
    a. She tells Gilly that Gilly's leaving is killing her
    b. She tells Gilly to make her proud.
    c. She tells Gilly that she will come and see her right away to be sure she is OK.
    d. Both a and b

17. How does her grandmother change after Gilly arrives?
    a. She wants Gilly to call her granny.
    b. She asks Gilly to wear Courtney's old clothes.
    c. She starts talking nonstop.
    d. She wants Gilly to have tea parties everyday at noon.

18. Miss Harris, Gilly's teacher from Thompson Park, sends Gilly
    a. the poem she wrote for her.
    b. a set of books by J.R. Tolkein.
    c. a picture of herself that resembled the cut-out magazine picture on the poem.
    d. a long letter telling Gilly about her anger.

The Great Gilly Hopkins Multiple Choice Unit Test 2 page5

19. Why is Gilly stunned and upset at the airport?
    a. Courtney looks nothing like her picture.
    b. Nonnie sent Courtney the money to fly home to see her.
    c. Courtney only plans to stay for two days.
    d. All of the above

20. How does Gilly deal with her fear and disappointment?
    a. She excuses herself to the bathroom and tries to throw up.
    b. She dials Trotter's number and begs her to let her to come home.
    c. She runs off as Courtney and Nonnie stand there watching her.
    d. Both a and b

The Great Gilly Hopkins Multiple Choice Unit Test 2 page 6

III. Quotations: Identify the speaker:

A= William Earnest   B= Mr. Randolph   C= Courtney   D= Gilly   E= Miss Harris

F= Miss Ellis   G=Nonnie   H= Trotter

1. "One thing we better get straight right now tonight. I won't have you making fun of that boy. One more thing. In this house we don't take the Lord's name in vain."

2. "Call me if you want anything. It ain't a shameful thing to need help, you know."

3. "That is probably exactly the flower that Mr. Wordsworth meant, sure is the lowliest flower of them all."

4. "I'm coming, Courtney, trailing clouds of glory as I come."

5. "Pow. I say, it sure fly good."

6. "You may find this hard to believe, Gilly, but you and I are very much alike. I don't mean in intelligence, although that is true, too. Both of us are smart, and we know it. But the thing that brings us closer than intelligence is anger. You and I are two of the angriest people I know. We do different things with our anger, of course. I was always taught to deny mine, which I did and still do. And that makes me envy you. Your anger is still up here on the surface where you can look it in the face, and make friends with it if you want."

7. "Oh, mercy, mercy. The boy is always looking for some excuse to say I can't take care of myself so he can drag me over to his big house in Virginia."

8. "Come home, Gilly. Please come home! Please, please!"

9. "You can't do that, Mrs. Trotter. You can't let them tear you to pieces. You're a foster mother and you can't afford to forget that."

10. "As a matter of fact, this letter- this letter is the first direct word we've - I've had from my daughter in thirteen years. I didn't even know she had a ba-"

11. "You bet I wouldn't. I don't understand why a smart girl like you goes around booby-trapping herself. You could have stayed here indefinitely, you know. They're both crazy about you."

The Great Gilly Hopkins Multiple Choice Unit Test 2 page 7

12. "She wanted something Trotter had no power over. To stop being a "foster child". To be real without any quotation marks. To belong and to possess."

13. "You make me proud, hear?"

14. "I told you on the phone that I'd come for Christmas and see for myself how the kid was doing... Look, I came, didn't I? Don't start pushing me before I'm hardly off the plane. My god, I've been gone thirteen years, and you still think you can tell me what to do."

15. "My sweet baby, ain't no one ever told you yet? I reckon I thought you had it all figured out. All that stuff about happy endings is lies. The only ending in this world is death. Now that might or might not be happy, but either way, you ain't ready to die, are you?"

The Great Gilly Hopkins Multiple Choice Unit Test 2 page 8
IV. Vocabulary (Matching)

____ 1. IMBECILE		A.	favorably
____ 2. FANATIC		B.	useless
____ 3. FUTILE		C.	brilliant
____ 4. FEEBLE		D.	endless
____ 5. RELENTLESSLY		E.	inability; failing
____ 6. PERPETUAL		F.	impressed deeply
____ 7. APPARITION		G.	maniac
____ 8. LEERING		H.	moron; dimwit
____ 9. KALEIDOSCOPIC		I.	trembling
____ 10. TRIFLED		J.	glaring
____ 11. ENGRAVED		K.	in an obeying manner
____ 12. INCOMPETENCE		L.	hug
____ 13. DELECTABLE		M.	ghost
____ 14. DELINQUENCY		N.	unsigned
____ 15. EMBRACE		O.	delicious
____ 16. OBLIGINGLY		P.	neglect; wrongdoing
____ 17. BENIGNLY		Q.	stretch
____ 18. EXPANSE		R.	weak
____ 19. ANONYMOUS		S.	toyed or played with
____ 20. QUAVERING		T.	steadily

ANSWER SHEET - *The Great Gilly Hopkins*
Multiple Choice Unit Tests

I. Matching	II. Multiple Choice	III. Quotes	IV. Vocabulary
1. ___	1. ___	1. ___	1. ___
2. ___	2. ___	2. ___	2. ___
3. ___	3. ___	3. ___	3. ___
4. ___	4. ___	4. ___	4. ___
5. ___	5. ___	5. ___	5. ___
6. ___	6. ___	6. ___	6. ___
7. ___	7. ___	7. ___	7. ___
8. ___	8. ___	8. ___	8. ___
9. ___	9. ___	9. ___	9. ___
10. ___	10. ___	10. ___	10. ___
11. ___	11. ___	11. ___	11. ___
12. ___	12. ___	12. ___	12. ___
13. ___	13. ___	13. ___	13. ___
14. ___	14. ___	14. ___	14. ___
15. ___	15. ___	15. ___	15. ___
	16. ___		16. ___
	17. ___		17. ___
	18. ___		18. ___
	19. ___		19. ___
	20. ___		20. ___

ANSWER KEY MULTIPLE CHOICE UNIT TESTS
The Great Gilly Hopkins

Answers to Unit Test 1 are in the left column. Answers to Unit Test 2 are in the right column.

I. Matching	II. Multiple Choice	III. Quotes	IV. Vocabulary
1. A K	1. B D	1. B G	1. I H
2. O M	2. B A	2. B G	2. L G
3. B N	3. C A	3. E B	3. Q B
4. F G	4. D C	4. A D	4. J R
5. N E	5. B D	5. C A	5. T T
6. G D	6. C B	6. H E	6. B D
7. J C	7. D A	7. E B	7. H M
8. I J	8. B B	8. C A	8. K J
9. H F	9. C D	9. D F	9. A C
10. K H	10. A C	10. F G	10. M S
11. C I	11. D B	11. D F	11. R F
12. L O	12. D C	12. A D	12. D E
13. M L	13. A B	13. B H	13. N O
14. D B	14. A D	14. G C	14. F P
15. E A	15. D B	15. B D	15. O L
	16. B D		16. E K
	17. C C		17. G A
	18. C B		18. C Q
	19. C D		19. P N
	20. D D		20. S I

UNIT RESOURCE MATERIALS

BULLETIN BOARD IDEAS - *The Great Gilly Hopkins*

1. Post students' Writing Assignment #1, Missing Posters, appealing for Gilly's return.

2. Bring in (or have students bring in) pictures of clouds, horses, decorated Christmas trees, sets of encyclopedias, stepladders, chandeliers, J.R. Tolkein books and/or his book characters, buses, bus station, suitcases, basketballs, airports, Vietnam War Era airplanes, etc. Make a collage if you have enough different pictures (or post individual pictures on colorful paper if you only have a few pictures). This could also be a fun introductory activity if students participate. You could have the border and title " A Journey Home" done for the bulletin board and invite students to staple up their own pictures wherever they want them. It will only take a few minutes of class time, but the students will enjoy it and you can get your bulletin board done in a hurry.

3. Draw one of the word search puzzles onto the bulletin board. (Be sure to enlarge it.) Write the key words to one side. Invite students to take their pens or markers and find the words before and/or after class (or perhaps this could be an activity for students who finish their work early).

4. Create a large, detailed illustration of how to fold and fly the perfect paper airplane. Staple up various student-made examples.

5. Have students generate their impression of the treasured portrait Gilly had of Courtney based on Gilly's descriptions of it from the novel.

6. Illustrate the main characters by silhouettes, portraits, or whatever your choice. Include information gained from the novel describing them.

7. Post the words to the poem by William Wordsworth. Have students illustrate according to their interpretation of the poem.

8. Make a mural depicting Thompson Park. Be sure to include the bus station, Trotter's house, Mr. Randolph's house, and the school. Make a contrasting mural of Jackson, Virginia, where Gilly moves with her grandmother.

9. Post any of the students' Writing Assignments, in addition to their Missing Posters. They could illustrate something from their Writing Assignment to enhance it.

10. Create a collage of art work from students that conveys their impressions of the characters in this story.

11. Post pictures of runners, races, track contests, Olympics, etc. Maybe students could make a graph of their running times from P.E. class.

EXTRA ACTIVITIES - *Great Gilly Hopkins*

One of the difficulties in teaching a novel is that all students don't read at the same speed. One student who likes to read may take the book home and finish it in a day or two. Sometimes a few students finish the in-class assignments early. The problem, then, is finding suitable extra activities for students.

The best idea is to keep a library in the classroom. For this unit on *The Great Gilly Hopkins*, you might check out from the school library other books by Katherine Paterson. A biography of the author would be interesting for some students, or J.R. Tolkein's Trilogy set may be of interest. You may include other related books and articles about: foster care, paper airplanes, racial discrimination, poetry, San Francisco, horses, Vietnam War, flower children, etc.

Keep puzzles on hand. We have made some relating directly to *The Great Gilly Hopkins* for you. Feel free to duplicate them for your students.

Some students may like to draw. You might devise a contest or allow some extra-credit grade for students who draw characters or scenes from *The Great Gilly Hopkins*. Note, too, that if the students do not want to keep their drawings you may pick up some extra bulletin board materials this way. If you have a contest and you supply the prize or, you could possibly make the drawing itself a non-refundable entry fee.

The pages which follow contain games, puzzles and worksheets. The keys, when appropriate, immediately follow the puzzle or worksheet. There are two main groups of activities: one group for the unit; that is, generally relating to *The Great Gilly Hopkins* text, and another group of activities related strictly to *The Great Gilly Hopkins* vocabulary.

Directions for the games, puzzles and worksheets are self-explanatory. The object here is to provide you with extra materials you may use in any way you choose.

MORE ACTIVITIES - *The Great Gilly Hopkins*

1. Pick a chapter or scene with a great deal of dialogue and have the students act it out on a stage. (Perhaps you could assign various scenes to different groups of students so more than one scene could be acted and more students could participate.)

2. Listen to the audio tape version of this novel. Have the students evaluate the voices used on the tape. Do they match what they imagined the characters would sound like as they read the book?

3. Have students design a book cover (front and back and inside flaps) for *The Great Gilly Hopkins*.

4. Students could write a sequel chapter that explains how Gilly gets along living in Virginia. Does Courtney stay?

5. Debate the advantages or disadvantages of living with a grandparent.

6. Use some of the related topics (noted earlier for an in-class library) as topics for research, reports or written papers, or as topics for guest speakers.

7. Have students plan and teach a lesson on a chapter or section of the book. Give them guidelines and a time frame.

8. Visit a foster home and interview the foster parents and children (if they agree).

9. Have a bubble blowing contest. Take pictures and post them. Vote on which one most closely resembles Gilly.

10. Write to Katherine Paterson asking her questions students have composed. You could send a class set of letters in one large envelope.

11. Construct a variety of paper airplanes. Have a paper airplane-throwing contest based on distance and height.

12. Research music, fashions, hairstyles, political sentiments, etc. of this era. There are many Post-Vietnam movies that reflect the political climate. Perhaps your students could research this topic and make a report to the class. This will help them better understand Courtney and Miss Harris' characters.

13. Create a cleaning-the-house chart. Have students compare their chores at home to those that Gilly was required to do or offered to do in her 'cleaning' streak.

More Activities - *The Great Gilly Hopkins* page 2

14. Invite a willing relative of your students in to share information about this time period, perhaps a Vietnam veteran.

15. Have students interview someone who lived during this time period (Post Vietnam Era), preferably a parent. Have students compose questions together for their interviews. They could then make a booklet with the information in it for display. Have them illustrate the cover with something they learned about the times from their interview.

16. Allow students to select a character from the novel. Have them dress like them, speak like them; assume their persona. Create a talk show format with these characters as the guests. Have a student volunteer to be the host. Others not involved will the audience, questioning the characters. One of your students could pretend to be a trained psychologist who comes out later in the show to help the panel solve their problems. Have a topic like: racial discrimination, sibling rivalry, i.e. problems encountered in the novel. Allow the class to decide as much as possible. Have questions from the audience ready prior to the show day. You could have students try out for the parts. Remind them to keep it on the up and up, not to mimic some of the seedier talk shows. This will require students to take an in-depth look into characterization in the novel.

17. View a filmstrip on Katherine Paterson.

18. Students who like board games may want to create one using information from this novel. Some students could work together as a group to complete this task. Encourage them to look at setting to illustrate their board and possibly use vocabulary, characters, plot, etc. for question cards.

19. Hold a poetry reading session. Invite parents and others to attend and to share original or published poetry. Be sure to include the reading of Wordsworth's poem.

20. Watch an episode of Sesame Street. Discuss why it would have been William Earnest's favorite show. Take a poll and create a graph that depicts your student's favorite shows.

21. Discuss ways to handle anger constructively, rather than by hurting others. Create a booklet that all members of the class can pull out and review when anger hits.

22. Invite a guidance counselor to address key issues inherent to this story such as: abandonment, foster care, living with grandparents, disappointment, anger, racial discrimination, etc. Reading a fictional portrayal of these issues will sometimes evoke emotional responses in your students.

23. Plan and prepare a meal like one that Trotter would have cooked. Serve and enjoy. Invite someone needy (like Mr. Randolph) to join you.

WORD SEARCH - *The Great Gilly Hopkins*

All the words in this list are associated with *The Great Gilly Hopkins*. The words are placed backwards, forward, diagonally, up and down. The words are listed below the word search.

```
X G S W O R D S W O R T H I R T Y - F O U R B C
V C O E M R . R A N D O L P H K T C Q T H W U C
P H B O S X C D F E B H X O Q B H A Y T Y T B J
Q A M H D A J W X T B D S R R F E L P W D V B T
J D M Q B B M Q C H M V Q A Z F N I Q Y U X L D
B W I P J N O E F I N R Q N W T E F N M L T E H
C E S B F T C O S R N M . G J R V O B H L V G S
B L S F Y K F B K T H R E E T H I R T E E N U Z
K L H D N L A O S Y R M D L V R N N E W S L M Q
H J A B E M N O P S S E I I V A S I S C T H P V
G A R C B F G K O I I O E S X I N A F E E E G Q
U C R F K S E S W X X N N T S O N S I T L S N W
A K I R L C R N W S T E O A J E N R V U A T S K
R S S K I U W V D I O - N M D K L S E T W V Z T
D O P R W S H B V X O W N P K K D L F U Y N P P
M N H L T L - Q M T N A I K X T W S I S E D Y H
T O L K E I N 6 V Y E Y E V M S R F K S R T M S
```

ANGER	HELP	RINSE
BLACK	JACKSON	SESAME STREET
BOOKS	LAWYER	SIX TO ONE
BUBBLE GUM	MELVIN	STAMP
CALIFORNIA	MISS ELLIS	TEN
CHADWELL	MISS HARRIS	THE NEVINS
DEFEND	MR. EVANS	THIRTEEN
DIXONS	MR. RANDOLPH	THIRTY-FOUR
DULLES	NONNIE	THREE
FIVE	ONE-WAY	TOLKEIN
FLU	ONE THIRTY- SIX SIXTY	TUTUS
GOOD BOOK	ORANGE	WORDSWORTH
GUARD	POW	
HARRIS-6	RECESS	

KEY: WORD SEARCH - *The Great Gilly Hopkins*

All the words in this list are associated with *The Great Gilly Hopkins*. The words are placed backwards, forward, diagonally, up and down. The words are listed below the word search.

```
          G S W O R D S W O R T H I R T Y - F O U R B
          C O E M R . R A N D O L P H     T C       U
          H   O S         E       O       H A       B
          A     D A       T       R       E L     D B
          D M       B M       H M       A     N I     U L
          W I         O E     I   R     N     E F     L E
          E S           O S R     M . G   R V O     H L G
        B L S           B K T H R E E T H I R T E E N   U
          L H D       A O   Y R M D L V   N N E       S L M
        H J A     E   N O P S S E I I V A S I     S C T     P
        G A R C     F G K O I I O E S X I N A F E E E
        U C R F K     E S W X X N N T S O N S I T L S       N
        A K I R L     R N   S T E O A     E N     V U A     S
        R S S   I U     D I O - N M       L S E T W
        D O         S         X O W N P         L   U Y
          N           -         T N A I             I S E
        T O L K E I N 6         Y E Y E                 S R
```

ANGER	HELP	RINSE
BLACK	JACKSON	SESAME STREET
BOOKS	LAWYER	SIX TO ONE
BUBBLE GUM	MELVIN	STAMP
CALIFORNIA	MISS ELLIS	TEN
CHADWELL	MISS HARRIS	THE NEVINS
DEFEND	MR. EVANS	THIRTEEN
DIXONS	MR. RANDOLPH	THIRTY-FOUR
DULLES	NONNIE	THREE
FIVE	ONE-WAY	TOLKEIN
FLU	ONE THIRTY- SIX SIXTY	TUTUS
GOOD BOOK	ORANGE	WORDSWORTH
GUARD	POW	
HARRIS-6	RECESS	

CROSSWORD - *The Great Gilly Hopkins*

CROSSWORD CLUES - *The Great Gilly Hopkins*

ACROSS

1. Foster home location in Maryland _____ Park
6. Mr. Randolph's son
8. Insists on no fighting at school: Mr. ____
10. Gilly was afraid to touch someone this color
12. Number of dollars Gilly Paid Agnes for assisting in plot
14. Gilly needed it to clean the chandelier
16. Gilly stuck it under left-hand car door handle
18. Author of books Miss Harris sent Gilly
19. Airport where Courtney arrives
20. East meals at Maime Trotter's; Mr. _____
24. Nonnie's new hair coloring job
25. Hundreds of them fill Mr. Randolph's house
26. Case worker for Gilly: Miss ___
27. Stolen from Trotter to send letter to Courtney

DOWN

1. Number of dollars that fell out of the encyclopedia
2. Hippopotamus of a woman: ___Trotter
3. W.E.'s favorite TV program; _____ St.
4. Gilly's most recent foster parents' the _____
5. Author
7. Bespectacled younger foster brother: _____ Earnest
9. Odds in playground fight; ___ to one
11. Courtney's brother who died in Vietnam
12. Virus all except Gilly caught around Thanksgiving
13. Nickname main character gives herself; _____ Gilly
15. W.E.'s favorite word
16. 11 year-old foster girl: ___ Hopkins
17. Trotter's deceased husband
18. Age when Gilly had seen her mother
19. Left Gilly and moved to Florida
21. Courtney's mother
22. Reading group W.E. got promoted to
23. Gilly wrote a poem for her

CROSSWORD ANSWER KEY - *The Great Gilly Hopkins*

```
. T H O M P S O N . . P . . . . L A W Y E R .
. E . A . E . E V A N S . . . I . . . . . .
. N . I . S . V . T . I . . B L A C K . . .
. . . M . A . I . E . X . . . L . H . . . .
. F I V E . M . N . R . . . . I . A . . . G
. L . . . E . S . S T E P L A D D E R . . R
G U M . . . . . . . O . O . . M . W . . . U
A . E . T O L K E I N . W . . . . E . . . E
L . L . H . . . . . . . D U L L E S . . . S
A . V . R A N D O L P H . I . . . L . . . O
D . I . E . O . . . R . . X . . . L . . . M
R I N S E . N . . . A . . . B O O K S . . E
I . . . . . N . . . R . . . N . . . . . . .
E L L I S . I . . . R . . . . . . S T A M P
L . . . . . E . . . I . . . . . . . . . . .
. . . . . . . . . . S . . . . . . . . . . .
```

141

MATCHING QUIZ/WORKSHEET 1 - *The Great Gilly Hopkins*

_____ 1. RINSE   A. For my beautiful Galadriel

_____ 2. AGNES STOKES B. Number of dollars Gilly paid Agnes for assisting

_____ 3. THOMPSON PARK C. Where the Nevins' live

_____ 4. MASTERPIECE   D. Nonnie's new hair coloring job

_____ 5. GALADRIEL HOPKINS E. Town in Virginia where Nonnie lives

_____ 6. TEN   F. Money that fell from behind encyclopedia

_____ 7. MR. RANDOLPH G. The Holy Bible

_____ 8. INSCRIPTION   H. What Gilly called her car to Miss Harris

_____ 9. GOOD BOOK   I. Lives with her grandmother

_____ 10. CLOUDS OF GLORY J. Nonnie's son who died in Vietnam

_____ 11. CHADWELL   K. Imaginary horse Gilly invents for W.E.

_____ 12. MAIME TROTTER L. Eats meals at Maime Trotter's

_____ 13. HOLLYWOOD GARDENS M. Type of ticket Gilly bought

_____ 14. HARRIS-6   N. Eleven year-old foster girl

_____ 15. FLOWER CHILD O. Insists on no fighting

_____ 16. HELP   P. What everyone was offering Gilly

_____ 17. JACKSON   Q. Foster home location in Maryland

_____ 18. MR. EVANS   R. Hippopotamus of a woman

_____ 19. ONE-WAY   S. Describes Courtney

_____ 20. FIVE   T. Gilly's new classroom

KEY: MATCHING QUIZ/WORKSHEET 1 - *The Great Gilly Hopkins*

D 1. RINSE   A. For my beautiful Galadriel

I 2. AGNES STOKES   B. Number of dollars Gilly paid Agnes for assisting

Q 3. THOMPSON PARK   C. Where the Nevins' live

H 4. MASTERPIECE   D. Nonnie's new hair coloring job

N 5. GALADRIEL HOPKINS   E. Town in Virginia where Nonnie lives

F 6. TEN   F. Money that fell from behind encyclopedia

L 7. MR. RANDOLPH   G. The Holy Bible

A 8. INSCRIPTION   H. What Gilly called her card to Miss Harris

G 9. GOOD BOOK   I. Lives with her grandmother

K 10. CLOUDS OF GLORY   J. Nonnie's son who died in Vietnam

J 11. CHADWELL   K. Imaginary horse Gilly invents for W.E.

R 12. MAIME TROTTER   L. Eats meals at Maime Trotter's

C 13. HOLLYWOOD GARDENS   M. Type of ticket Gilly bought

T 14. HARRIS-6   N. Eleven year-old foster girl

S 15. FLOWER CHILD   O. Insists on no fighting

P 16. HELP   P. What everyone was offering Gilly

E 17. JACKSON   Q. Foster home location in Maryland

O 18. MR. EVANS   R. Hippopotamus of a woman

M 19. ONE-WAY   S. Describes Courtney

B 20. FIVE   T. Gilly's new classroom

MATCHING QUIZ/WORKSHEET 2 - *The Great Gilly Hopkins*

____ 1. THIRTEEN

____ 2. THE NEVINS

____ 3. STEPLADDER

____ 4. GRUESOME GILLY

____ 5. THREE

____ 6. GUARD

____ 7. NATIONAL APTITUDE

____ 8. AGNES STOKES

____ 9. FLOWER CHILD

____ 10. TEN

____ 11. COURTNEY R HOPKINS

____ 12. DIXONS

____ 13. HOLLYWOOD GARDENS

____ 14. STAMP

____ 15. RINSE

____ 16. FLU

____ 17. MASTERPIECE

____ 18. THIRTY-FOUR

____ 19. ANGER

____ 20. TUTUS

A. Emotion that Miss Harris and Gilly share

B. Virus all except Gilly on Thanksgiving

C. Money that fell from behind encyclopedia

D. Nickname main character gives herself

E. Needed to clean chandelier

F. Mother who abandons Gilly

G. Left Gilly and moved to Florida

H. Test Gilly scored highest on

I. Nonnie's new hair coloring job

J. Where the Nevins 'live

K. Age when Gilly had last seen her mother

L. What Gilly called her card to Miss Harris

M. Role Agnes played in theft of money

N. Gilly's most recent foster home

O. Amount of money W.E. found for Gilly

P. Ballerinas on Melvin's tie wore these

Q. Lives with her grandmother

R. Stolen from Trotter to mail letter to Courtney

S. Years since Nonnie heard from Courtney

T. Describes Courtney

KEY: MATCHING QUIZ/WORKSHEET 2 - *The Great Gilly Hopkins*

S   1. THIRTEEN   A. Emotion that Miss Harris and Gilly share

N   2. THE NEVINS   B. Virus all except Gilly got on Thanksgiving

E   3. STEPLADDER   C. Money that fell from behind encyclopedia

D   4. GRUESOME GILLY   D. Nickname main character gives herself

K   5. THREE   E. Needed to clean chandelier

M 6. GUARD   F. Mother who abandons Gilly

H   7. NATIONAL APTITUDE   G. Left Gilly and moved to Florida

Q 8. AGNES STOKES   H. Test Gilly scored highest on

T   9. FLOWER CHILD   I.   Nonnie's new hair coloring job

C 10. TEN   J.   Where the Nevins' live

F   11. COURTNEY R HOPKINS   K. Age when Gilly had last seen her mother

G 12. DIXONS   L.   What Gilly called her card to Miss Harris

J   13. HOLLYWOOD GARDENS   M. Role Agnes played in theft of money

R 14. STAMP   N. Gilly's most recent foster home

I   15. RINSE   O. Amount of money W.E. found for Gilly

B 16. FLU   P. Ballerinas on Melvin's tie wore these

L   17. MASTERPIECE   Q. Lives with her grandmother

O 18. THIRTY-FOUR   R. Stolen from Trotter to mail letter to Courtney

A 19. ANGER   S. Ysince Nonnie heard from Courtney

P 20. TUTUS   T. Describes Courtney

JUGGLE LETTER REVIEW GAME CLUE SHEET - *The Great Gilly Hopkins*

SCRAMBLED	WORD	CLUE
EASDRPDELT	STEPLADDER	Needed to clean chandelier
AIRNSFCASOCN	SAN FRANCISCO	Gilly's destination
-WNOEYA	ONE-WAY	Type of ticket Gilly bought
IAMRSSSHIR	MISS HARRIS	Poem is written for her
OOBOOGKD	GOOD BOOK	The Holy Bible
IVNLEM	MELVIN	Trotter's deceased husband
OSKOB	BOOKS	Hundreds of them fill Mr. Randolph's house
UELSDL	DULLES	Airport Courtney flew in to
SEILLISSM	MISS ELLIS	Caseworker for Gilly
UFL	FLU	Virus all except Gilly got on Thanksgiving
RRH6S-AI	HARRIS-6	Gilly's new classroom
NRIES	RINSE	Nonnie's new hair coloring job
EPLNEPAARARPI	PAPER AIRPLANE	It sure fly good
ECSSER	RECESS	Where Gilly takes basketball away
KNOSAJC	JACKSON	Town in Virginia where Nonnie lives
EEOANTSSGKS	AGNES STOKES	Lives with her grandmother
ADRGU	GUARD	Role Agnes played in theft of money
DPH.MARLRNO	MR.RANDOLPH	Eats meals at Maime Trotter's
WLOYNLODGERSDOHA	HOLLYWOOD GARDENS	Where the Nevins'live
IERIMALLNSTWEA	WILLIAM EARNEST	Bespectacled younger foster brother
PTMAOKHOSNPR	THOMPSON PARK	Foster home location in Maryland
IPTTATNUNDIAOEL	NATIONAL APTITUDE	Test Gilly scored highest on
DEENFD	DEFEND	W.E. learns to do this from Gilly
ASMNRV.E	MR. EVANS	Insists on no fighting
NAIROCFALI	CALIFORNIA	Postmark on Courtney's postcard
ENT	TEN	Money that fell from behind encyclopedia
IOREARTMEMTT	MAIMETROTTER	Hippopotamus of a woman
STUTU	TUTUS	Ballerinas on Melvin's tie wore these
NONRITCISPI	INSCRIPTION	For my beautiful Galadriel
KRYRONCOPUHSTNIE	COURTNEY R HOPKINS	Mother who abandons Gilly
EOOISNXT	SIX TO ONE	Odds in playground fight
ISLILSESM	MISS ELLIS	Caseworker for Gilly
SIXTEOIITNYHXSYRT	ONE THIRTY- SIX SIXTY	Price of one-way ticket to San Francisco

VOCABULARY RESOURCE MATERIALS

VOCABULARY WORD SEARCH - *The Great Gilly Hopkins*

All the words in this list are associated with *The Great Gilly Hopkins* with emphasis on the vocabulary words being studied in the unit. The words are placed backwards, forward, diagonally, up and down. The words are listed below the word search.

```
I N E X O R A B L Y Y B O T R I F L E D P C F C
N C N N T N R R Y R D E I B C S G A U D I E S T
C O G F G Z T Q K I H N M F L Z V B M K R C Y H
O N R W S U W D T F A I B N C I B O R R N U Z T
M F A O T F L J Q F U G E T J A G R G C F L F B
P I V E R X Q F Z L D N C S L S N I G N E I L T
E R E F I O W U E E I L I E J A B O N D E N I X
T M D U C B P F A D B Y L E B L D U P G B A R F
E E T L K S F G R V L C E T V V B S Y I L R T P
N D E L E C T A B L E N T H R A L L E D E Y A T
C H X Y N E H D E F X R S E N G P Y E S M D T M
E Z H F S N F N M A P T I D F E I K V E L Y I C
L D F R U I Q M B N A A S N C L O D L X R N O R
A N O I N T E D R A N R G W G C U H E F T I N G
V G D N T Y I X A T S M X O F C S T K N P M N L
F F S Q Y B B L C I E S F Z N L L S E F R Q J G
F R A C A S B N E C L A D E N Y Y C R D R P T D
```

AGONY	ENGULFED	HEFTING	QUAVERING
ANOINTED	ENTHRALLED	IMBECILE	RIFFLED
AUDIBLE	EXPANSE	INCOMPETENCE	SALVAGE
BENIGNLY	FANATIC	INEXORABLY	SEETHED
CANOPIED	FEEBLE	LABORIOUSLY	STRICKEN
CONFIRMED	FLIRTATION	LADEN	TRIFLED
CULINARY	FLUTED	LEERING	WOEFULLY
DELECTABLE	FRACAS	OBLIGINGLY	
EMBRACE	FUTILE	OBSCENITY	
ENGRAVED	GAUDIEST	PIOUSLY	

KEY: VOCABULARY WORD SEARCH - *The Great Gilly Hopkins*

All the words in this list are associated with *The Great Gilly Hopkins* with emphasis on the vocabulary words being studied in the unit. The words are placed backwards, forward, diagonally, up and down. The words are listed below the word search.

```
    I N E X O R A B L Y     B O T R I F L E D
  N C N                 R   E I B       G A U D I E S T
    C O G     G         I   N M   L     B           C
    O N R W S U         F A I B   C I   O           U
    M F A O T   L       F U G E     A G R       F L F
    P I V E R   Q F     L D N C S   S N I       E I L
    E R E F I O   U E E I L I E     A   O N     E N I
    T M D U C B     A D B Y L E     L   U P G B A R
    E E   L K S       V L E T   V   S     I L R T
    N D E L E C T A B L E N T H R A L L E D E Y A
    C       Y N E     E F X R   E   G P Y E     D T
    E       F N       M A P   I D F E I     E     I
            U I       B N A A   N   L O         R O
    A N O I N T E D R A N   G   G   U H E F T I N G
              Y I     A T S     O   S T           N
                  L C I E       N   L   E         G
    F R A C A S       E C L A D E N Y Y     D
```

AGONY	ENGULFED	HEFTING	QUAVERING
ANOINTED	ENTHRALLED	IMBECILE	RIFFLED
AUDIBLE	EXPANSE	INCOMPETENCE	SALVAGE
BENIGNLY	FANATIC	INEXORABLY	SEETHED
CANOPIED	FEEBLE	LABORIOUSLY	STRICKEN
CONFIRMED	FLIRTATION	LADEN	TRIFLED
CULINARY	FLUTED	LEERING	WOEFULLY
DELECTABLE	FRACAS	OBLIGINGLY	
EMBRACE	FUTILE	OBSCENITY	
ENGRAVED	GAUDIEST	PIOUSLY	

VOCABULARY CROSSWORD - *The Great GillyHopkins*

VOCABULARY CROSSWORD CLUES - *The Great Gilly Hopkins*

ACROSS
3. Toyed or played with
7. Raged; fumed
9. In an obeying manner
14. Changed; distracted
16. Rescue; save
17. Useless
19. Misery
22. Favorably
24. Decoratively covered between bedposts
27. Weak
29. Flooded
30. Can be heard

DOWN
1. Searched
2. In a holy manner
4. Collection
5. Having grooves
6. Neglect; wrongdoing
8. Intensely
10. Predatory fish
11. Flashiest
12. Lifting
13. With great detail
15. Revenge
16. Pure
18. Unsigned; unknown
20. Swearing
21. Fascinated
23. Dedicated
25. Dimwit; moron
26. Troubled
27. Uproar
28. Loaded down

VOCABULARY CROSSWORD ANSWER KEY - *The Great GillyHopkins*

VOCABULARY WORKSHEET 1 - *The Great Gilly Hopkins*

___ 1. LEERING   A.   hug

___ 2. VARIATIONS   B.   impressed deeply

___ 3. APPALLING   C.   therapists

___ 4. DELECTABLE   D.   collection

___ 5. EXPANSE   E.   searched

___ 6. RIFFLED   F.   inability; failing

___ 7. REPERTORY   G.   hearable

___ 8. TRIFLED   H.   variety

___ 9. PSYCHOLOGISTS   I.   trembling

___ 10. STRICKEN   J.   toyed or played with

___ 11. QUAVERING   K.   pure

___ 12. SELF-RIGHTEOUS   L.   proved

___ 13. CONFIRMED   M.   shocking

___ 14. AUDIBLE   N.   glaring

___ 15. LABORIOUSLY   O.   with great difficulty

___ 16. FANATIC   P.   delicious

___ 17. EMBRACE   Q.   maniac

___ 18. ENGRAVED   R.   troubled

___ 19. KALEIDOSCOPIC   S.   stretch

___ 20. INCOMPETENCE   T.   brilliant

KEY: VOCABULARY WORKSHEET 1 - *The Great Gilly Hopkins*

N	1. LEERING	A. hug
H	2. VARIATIONS	B. impressed deeply
M	3. APPALLING	C. therapists
P	4. DELECTABLE	D. collection
S	5. EXPANSE	E. searched
E	6. RIFFLED	F. inability; failing
D	7. REPERTORY	G. hearable
J	8. TRIFLED	H. variety
C	9. PSYCHOLOGISTS	I. trembling
R	10. STRICKEN	J. toyed or played with
I	11. QUAVERING	K. pure
K	12. SELF-RIGHTEOUS	L. proved
L	13. CONFIRMED	M. shocking
G	14. AUDIBLE	N. glaring
O	15. LABORIOUSLY	O. with great difficulty
Q	16. FANATIC	P. delicious
A	17. EMBRACE	Q. maniac
B	18. ENGRAVED	R. troubled
T	19. KALEIDOSCOPIC	S. stretch
F	20. INCOMPETENCE	T. brilliant

VOCABULARY WORKSHEET 2 - *The Great Gilly Hopkins*

___ 1. TENTATIVELY   A.   maniac

___ 2. ELABORATELY   B.   loaded down

___ 3. FANATIC   C.   lifting

___ 4. SUBMISSION   D.   revenge

___ 5. QUAVERING   E.   predatory fish

___ 6. KALEIDOSCOPIC   F.   brilliant

___ 7. IMBECILE   G.   misery

___ 8. BARRACUDA   H.   moron; dimwit

___ 9. FEEBLE   I.   inability; failing

___ 10. TRIFLED   J.   weak

___ 11. INCOMPETENCE   K.   rescue; save

___ 12. AGONY   L.   intensely

___ 13. EMBROIDERED   M.   toyed or played with

___ 14. EMPHATICALLY   N.   trembling

___ 15. HEFTING   O.   with uncertainty

___ 16. LADEN   P.   with great detail

___ 17. VARIATIONS   Q.   variety

___ 18. SEETHED   R.   having needlework

___ 19. SALVAGE   S.   meekness; surrender

___ 20. VENGEANCE   T.   raged; fumed

KEY: VOCABULARY WORKSHEET 2 - *The Great Gilly Hopkins*

O	1. TENTATIVELY	A.	maniac
P	2. ELABORATELY	B.	loaded down
A	3. FANATIC	C.	lifting
S	4. SUBMISSION	D.	revenge
N	5. QUAVERING	E.	predatory fish
F	6. KALEIDOSCOPIC	F.	brilliant
H	7. IMBECILE	G.	misery
E	8. BARRACUDA	H.	moron; dimwit
J	9. FEEBLE	I.	inability; failing
M	10. TRIFLED	J.	weak
I	11. INCOMPETENCE	K.	rescue; save
G	12. AGONY	L.	intensely
R	13. EMBROIDERED	M.	toyed or played with
L	14. EMPHATICALLY	N.	trembling
C	15. HEFTING	O.	with uncertainty
B	16. LADEN	P.	with great detail
Q	17. VARIATIONS	Q.	variety
T	18. SEETHED	R.	having needlework
K	19. SALVAGE	S.	meekness; surrender
D	20. VENGEANCE	T.	raged; fumed

VOCABULARY JUGGLE LETTER REVIEW GAME CLUES - *The Great Gilly Hopkins*

SCRAMBLED	WORD	CLUE
TEYLLLSEENSR	RELENTLESSLY	steadily
EDALIUB	AUDIBLE	hearable
SACRAF	FRACAS	uproar
H-ESGSEOTFIULR	SELF-RIGHTEOUS	pure
LEUAPPRTE	PERPETUAL	endless
INTCESRK	STRICKEN	troubled
IVGRAUNQE	QUAVERING	trembling
TEELLRHDAN	ENTHRALLED	fascinated
NLBYIGNE	BENIGNLY	favorably
EESDETH	SEETHED	raged; fumed
INLGPLAPA	APPALLING	shocking
ARYUCLIN	CULINARY	concerning cooking
LTIYIITBRAIR	IRRITABILITY	testiness
LLCTEEBDEA	DELECTABLE	delicious
FHIETGN	HEFTING	lifting
IOSINMSBUS	SUBMISSION	meekness; surrender
OARIAPIPNT	APPARITION	ghost
DGANREVE	ENGRAVED	deeply impressed
AAFICTN	FANATIC	maniac
OEXRIAYLNB	INEXORABLY	unable to stop
NITEBYCSO	OBSCENITY	swearing
EYEQUINLCND	DELINQUENCY	neglect; wrongdoing
LIYGELNTLREBE	BELLIGERENTLY	with hostility
RTFINILTAO	FLIRTATION	teasing
ONYAG	AGONY	misery
ECMLBEII	IMBECILE	dimwit; moron
ADENL	LADEN	loaded down
EDDMERERBOI	EMBROIDERED	having needlework
OLUWFYEL	WOEFULLY	sadly
VASEGLA	SALVAGE	save; rescue
UISAOLROYBL	LABORIOUSLY	with great difficulty
DFEUTL	FLUTED	having grooves